SYMMETRY AND SENSE

The Poetry of Sir Philip Sidney

SYMMETRY AND SENSE

The Poetry of Sir Philip Sidney

BY ROBERT L. MONTGOMERY, JR.

GREENWOOD PRESS, PUBLISHERS
NEW YORK

In Memoriam

George A. Everett
Hyder E. Rollins

Contents

SYMMETRY AND SENSE

The Poetry of Sir Philip Sidney

Foreword

$\mathcal{T}$he genesis of this book was my dissertation at Harvard under the guidance of Professors Herschel Baker, Douglas Bush, and Hyder Rollins. At various stages of the study each of them gave invaluable advice. I am further indebted to Professor Baker for a reading of my manuscript in its later forms and to Professors Thomas P. Harrison and Dewitt Starnes for their courtesy in reading the final version.

My thanks are due to staff members of the Houghton Library at Harvard and of the University of Texas Library for their kindness and diligence in assisting my work. Finally, I acknowledge with gratitude the research grants of the Research Institute of the University of Texas, which made possible the preparation of the manuscript.

The problem of choosing a text for Sidney's verse is a difficult one. Albert Feuillerat's *The Complete Works of Sir Philip Sidney* (4 vols., Cambridge, 1921–1929) brings all the poems together and is usually satisfactory for the *Lady of May* poems, the translations of the *Psalms,* and the *Arcadia* poems. But Feuillerat's error in choosing Thomas Newman's unauthorized and erroneous 1591 quarto as his text for *Astrophel and Stella* renders his edition of that work useless as a basis for criticism. In the absence of any really satisfactory modern edition of the sonnet sequence and the *Certaine Sonets,* I have gone to Ponsonby's 1598 folio, *The Countesse of Pembrokes Arcadia,* for my citations of those two collections.

Austin, Texas

1.

Introduction

*I*f we can credit his own testimony, Sidney valued poetry as the first and finest of arts but thought his own production trivial, no better than a "splendid toying." On the one hand he praises literary art as a better teacher than philosophy and on the other remarks that his own status as a poet is accidental. Years after his death his friend Fulke Greville appears to have agreed, for his memoir dwells almost exclusively on Sidney the man and the statesman, virtually ignoring Sidney the artist. And Greville was not alone. The rash of posthumous tributes to Sidney glamorized the images of the learned statesman and selfless warrior, making them public legend, and this emphasis all but overwhelms the occasional comments on his quality as a poet. The motives for such reticence are, of course, familiar. Poetry, for all its glory in the eyes of the Renaissance, was, like philosophy or history, a discipline in the service of ethics, an instrument of precept and example and a vehicle for the encouragement of right reason. Interest in art sooner or later arrived at an interest in its moral relevance, and a corollary to this view is the fact that poetry, not the work of a poet, was the target of all but the most fragmentary critical commentary.

1

It is difficult, then, to approach Sidney through the opinions of his contemporaries and near successors, and the Renaissance record is also unilluminating to any attempt to read Sidney's work as a mirror of his personality. Yet, until recent years, such has been the main endeavor of much of the criticism and scholarship devoted to him. Beginning with Pollard, Grosart, and Sir Sidney Lee, two generations of scholars have argued inconclusively over the relevance of *Astrophel and Stella* to events in Sidney's private life, using their findings as a basis for praising the "sincerity" of the work or dismissing it as "conventional" and unoriginal.[1] The issue of the genesis of *Astrophel and Stella* in the circumstances of Sidney's life has not yet been properly settled, and in any case it is a marginal problem so far as criticism of his verse is concerned. In addition, the quarrel and the assumptions upon which it is based have done Sidney's work a real disservice. They have meant the relative neglect of the *Arcadia* poems, the translations of the *Psalms*, and most of the miscellaneous poems collected by Sidney's sister and printed under the title *Certaine Sonets*.

With some exceptions more recent criticism of Sidney has also tended to dwell on the sonnet sequence, but it has at least sought more convincing grounds for evaluation. The comments of Theodore Spencer and Hallett Smith appear to be influenced by the efforts of the new

[1] A. W. Pollard, ed., *Sir Philip Sidney's Astrophel and Stella* (London, 1888), pp. viii–xxx, and A. B. Grosart, ed., *The Complete Poems of Sir Philip Sidney* (London, 1877), I, xlviii–lxviii, both accept Stella as Penelope Devereux. Sir Sidney Lee, *Great Englishmen of the Sixteenth Century* (New York, 1904), pp. 77–82, reads *Astrophel and Stella* as artificial, conventional Platonism. Later documents arguing for the autobiographical interpretation of the sequence are: Ewald Flügel, ed., *Sir Philip Sidney's* ASTROPHEL AND STELLA *und* DEFENCE OF POESIE (Halle, 1889), pp. l–li; Mona Wilson, ed., *Astrophel & Stella* (London, 1931), pp. xxvi–xxvii; Janet G. [Espiner-] Scott, *Les sonnets élisabéthains* (Paris, 1929), pp. 20–21; Hoyt H. Hudson, "Penelope Devereux as Sidney's Stella," *Huntington Library Bulletin*, VII (1935), 89–129; Lisle C. John, *The Elizabethan Sonnet Sequences* (New York, 1938), pp. 179–188; and Michel Poirier, *Sir Philip Sidney, le chevalier poète élisabéthain* (Lille, 1948), pp. 58–72. Documents arguing against this interpretation are: J. B. Fletcher, "Did Astrophel Love Stella?" *MP*, V (1907), 253–264, reprinted in *The Religion of Beauty in Women* (New York, 1911), pp. 147–165; James M. Purcell, *Sidney's Stella* (New York, 1934), pp. 43–72; T. H. Banks, "Sidney's *Astrophel and Stella* Reconsidered," *PMLA*, L (1935), 403–412; W. G. Friedrich, "The 'Stella' of 'Astrophel,'" *ELH*, III (1936), 114–139. A surprisingly recent commentary that accuses Sidney of shallow artificiality is in Odette de Mourges' *Metaphysical, Baroque, & Precieux Poetry* (Oxford, 1953), pp. 12–19.

critics at close stylistic investigation, and both men, together with Yvor Winters, C. S. Lewis, J. W. Lever, and Richard B. Young, have gone some distance in reading Sidney according to the literary canons of his own age.[2] These critics have ignored or subordinated the issues that bothered the biographical scholars and have drawn attention more and more to the problems of Sidney's technique. Spencer's important essay seeks to examine the range of Sidney's style as a continuous growth. Smith and Lever view his work in the sonnet against the background of the poets he followed, and they provide a number of concise and suggestive analyses of specific poems. Winters and Lewis, tracing Elizabethan lyric style in its historical development over a considerable lapse of time, are necessarily summary, but Young's monograph on *Astrophel and Stella,* the first really extended critique of the structure of the sequence, has done much to relieve the deficiencies of generalized comment. But of these critics Winters, for all the idiosyncracies of his views, offers the most useful framework for a comprehensive treatment of Sidney's style.

This is so because Winters refers his criticism to the rhetorical theories of the Renaissance and their influence on verse styles, and it is analysis of the rhetoric of Sidney's poems that still remains to be done. Except for Veré Rubel's description of some of Sidney's rhetorical figures,[3] the details of his use of rhetoric have been largely neglected, and, what is perhaps more important, the conjunction of rhetoric, other principles of rhythm, and the structure of imagery demand attention. Rhetorical criticism, although it has sometimes been overused, has the value of allowing the critic to start at the point where

[2] Yvor Winters, "The 16th Century Lyric in English," Parts I–II, *Poetry,* LIII (1939), 258–272, 320–335; Theodore Spencer, "The Poetry of Sir Philip Sidney," *ELH,* XII (1945), 251–278; Hallett Smith, *Elizabethan Poetry: A Study in Conventions, Meaning, and Expression* (Cambridge, Massachusetts, 1952), pp. 142–157; C. S. Lewis, *English Literature in the Sixteenth Century Excluding Drama* (Oxford, 1954), pp. 327–330; J. W. Lever, *The Elizabethan Love Sonnet* (London, 1956), pp. 51–91; Richard B. Young, *English Petrarke: A Study of Sidney's* ASTROPHEL AND STELLA in *Three Studies in the Renaissance,* Yale Studies in English, Vol. 138 (New Haven, 1958).

[3] *Poetic Diction in the English Renaissance from Skelton through Spenser,* Modern Language Association of America Revolving Fund Series, XII (New York, 1941). Of some interest also are Brother Simon Scribner's *Figures of Word-Repetition in Sir Philip Sidney's Arcadia* (Washington, D.C., 1948) and P. A. Duhamel's article, "Sidney's *Arcadia* and Elizabethan Rhetoric," *SP,* XLV (1948), 134–150.

the Renaissance was most explicit about its own literary art, and in Sidney's case it allows us to test his style according to standards he himself articulates.

Broadly speaking, Winters divides English poetry into two styles, the ornate and the plain. The ornate is epitomized in the "decadence" of Spenser—and of Sidney, for Winters allows him only an occasional plain poem; the plain in such poets as Wyatt, Raleigh, and especially Ben Jonson. Winters thinks the plain style better and more suited to the English genius because it is morally and rationally more responsible, but even without such a preference the categories are useful because they mirror the fundamental concerns of Renaissance thinking about style.

One kind of prose and verse style, the ornate, derives its authority from the purist imitators of Cicero and favors verbal abundance and ample rhythmical symmetry. It is a style of embellishment and overstatement, and in most respects it suits the emotional temperature of Petrarchan love poetry very well. The stately symmetry and hyperbole of Spenser is founded in large part on a mastery of the formulas of extended and intricate repetition, but the inept Petrarchan translations of Watson and the stale exercises of Tofte and a host of other minor figures are no less indebted to the long tradition of Ciceronian imitation. It is almost true to say that a decorative and abundant style is the dominant mode of Elizabethan verse in the latter two decades of the sixteenth century, reflecting the pressure of contemporary rhetorical training and an esthetic that persistently defines the poet as analogous to the orator. *The Arte of English Poesie,* that residuary of so much that is typical of Elizabethan opinion and practice, articulates these points specifically. Puttenham says, "Our maker or Poet is appointed not for a iudge, but rather for a pleader." And he describes the poet's style as the "richest attire" rather than "plaine and simple apparell."[4] The welter of illustrative quotation in the work fully confirms these views.

The plain style is associated with the reaction of another school of rhetoricians against Ciceronianism (but not necessarily against Cicero himself), a reaction that gathered force in Europe as early as Erasmus'

---

[4] *The Arte of English Poesie* (1589), ed. Gladys D. Willcock and Alice Walker (Cambridge, 1936), pp. 154, 137. All references to Puttenham are to this edition.

4

Ciceronianus (1528) but found its real power in the prose styles of
Lipsius, Montaigne, and Bacon and in the verse of Ben Jonson. In
technique the plain style opposes restraint and understatement to ornateness, the appearance of natural expression to the appearance of
artifice. It derives from an esthetic boasting a casual, spontaneous
effect, denying the validity of obvious and stylized ornament with the
excuse that ornament prevents clarity of idea. And the quarrel between
the advocates of the impromptu and the openly formal in language
goes deeper than preferences for different kinds of expression, for,
as George Williamson says, "It raised once more the old quarrel between philosophy and rhetoric, which in terms of style meant the essay
or plain style as opposed to the oratorical or grand style."[5]

For poetry the significance of this division has not always been clear.
Plain stylists cannot be said to abandon all concern for rhetorical problems, nor do they write (as they sometimes profess) straight from the
heart without attention to poetic convention. The "natural" order of
style is as much a product of artifice as any other. On the other side, a
poet of Spenser's caliber cannot be justly accused of neglecting the
sententious or moral substance of his verse. Furthermore, rhetorical
theory derived from prose has to be modified somewhat to describe the
styles of verse, which always has a more concentrated and highly
rhythmical foundation. Verse begins with an order of rhythm which
only the most highly artificial prose ever reaches. And finally there is
the problem of distinguishing sixteenth- and seventeenth-century verse
on rhetorical and logical grounds. The notion has long persisted that

[5] *The Senecan Amble* (Chicago, 1951), p. 12. Williamson (p. 59)
summarizes the range of prose styles as follows: "If discourse begins with the
psychological order, in which thought is allowed to run on just as it passes
through the mind, its first form is colloquial discourse, which has an emergent
order, the loosest of construction, the least committed syntax. Hence a conver-
sational style may be said to sacrifice the psychological order as little as possible
to logical and grammatical requirements, not at all to rhetorical order. At the
other extreme is the periodic style, which satisfies all these demands and culti-
vates the most ordered movement or rhythm." The discrimination of two general classes of style was commonplace: one was fit for reasoning and the other,
more formal and ornate, for oratorical persuasion. Thomas Wilson remarks
that logic "doth plainly and nakedlie set forthe with apte woordes, the summe
of thynges, by the waie of argumentacion," while rhetoric "useth gaie painted
sentences . . . at large" (*The Rule of Reason* [1567], sig. B3). Wilson here
points to a plain style one step removed in formality from Williamson's
"psychological order."

the poets of Elizabeth's reign were a nest of singing, and unphilo-
sophical, birds, entirely lacking in the intellectual strength of the
Metaphysicals.[6] It is true enough that from Jonson on a plainer style
emerged more generally than it had before, and it is also true that the
plain style proved more suitable to verse that imitated the mind in the
act of thinking. But the corollary that the ornateness of the sixteenth
century was a symptom of joyous or melancholy mindlessness is not
true. It is more important to note that, although the gaudiness of the
age of Elizabeth is reflected in the habits of ingenuity and verbal
abundance of many of its poets, there was still room for the flowering
of the tendencies we prize in Jonson on the one hand and in the Metaphysicals on the other. Moreover, the practice of the plain style, as
Winters reminds us, was a strong native tradition well before the time
of Elizabeth, and it was strengthened by Sidney's example to those
artists who imitated more than his adaptations of Petrarchan formulae.

Sidney's place in this context is somewhat complicated and it is
ambiguous in more than one sense. On the level of influence his work
is partially responsible for much that is unattractive in Petrarchan
imitations; both the *Arcadia* poems and the sequence lend themselves
to superficial mannerisms in minor and uncritical talents. On the
other hand, George Herbert surely learned a great deal of value from
Sidney, following his lead in stanzaic variety and what Louis Martz
calls neatness of structure.[7] Even more to the point is the fact that
Sidney's own style is a mixed one, sometimes predominantly ornate,
sometimes mostly plain, but seldom absolutely one or another. Quite
apart from specific influences, which are usually difficult to trace with
any certainty, he is a poet whose work epitomizes and illuminates the
major forces in Renaissance lyric style.

It is the central purpose of this book to locate and describe the
ornate and plain styles in Sidney's poems and to suggest where each
begins and ends. But, although the early poems are heavily ornate, I
do not study the relationship of these styles as a progress in time from

---

[6] I suspect this view is related to the current interest in the relations between
poetry and music. For example, Bruce Pattison, *Music and Poetry of the English Renaissance* (London, 1948), p. 142, generalizes: "The Elizabethan lyric
before Donne is always 'simple, sensuous and passionate.' Complex association
of idea, subtle play of wit, the poetic resources music cannot hope to copy, are
almost absent from it."

[7] *The Poetry of Meditation* (New Haven, 1954), pp. 266, 268.

amateur beginnings to professional achievement. The view that the *Arcadia* poems are apprentice experimentation succeeded by the maturity of *Astrophel and Stella* is too crude, and it is largely discredited by the evidence of continuing ornateness in the sequence. Furthermore, several of the *Arcadia* poems were revised after the sequence was completed and without damage to the esthetic impulse which originally set their style. Finally, there is some reason to think that Sidney's translations of the *Psalms*, in many respects close to the technique of the *Arcadia* poems, may have been his latest efforts.[8] The pattern of Sidney's talent, then, is not so much one of transition from one style to another as it is an adjustment of different styles to different purposes, even within the same poem or group of poems. If ornateness dominates the *Arcadia* verse, it exists in tension with a more incisive expression in *Astrophel and Stella,* and this tension is anything but the expression of a confused poetic aim. It reveals instead two divergent and conflicting points of view which extend to the dramatic structure of the whole of the sequence: Astrophel is torn between the ceremonial worship of his mistress and the melancholy, skeptical explorations of his own mind. And if styles reveal attitudes, these attitudes in their turn spring from familiar literary and ethical conventions deliberately used.

Love is the recurrent focus of Sidney's poems. This is conventional enough and would seem to limit his verse rather severely. The Arcadian world is sufficiently spacious to house other lyric subjects, but Sidney, with a few exceptions, has lovers speak his lines and more than demonstrates his obligation to the half-Platonic, half-Petrarchan tradition of idealistic and idealized emotion. Both the *Arcadia* poems and *Astrophel and Stella* gravitate to the mystique of the worship of women, even when, as in the *Arcadia,* some of the canons of Petrarchism are ignored, or, as in the sequence and some of the *Certaine Sonets,* its quasi-religious foundations are specifically challenged. But this singularity is not so lopsided as it seems. Even without his translations of the *Psalms* to balance the ledger, the traditions in which he works are broad enough to admit many conditions of mind and to tolerate the ambiguity of two dominant and opposed styles.

That this ambiguity is first of all revealed in distinct rhetorical purposes suggests the value of a rhetorically oriented criticism of Sidney's

[8] See Chapter 2, note 2.

verse. If the nearly compulsive interest of Renaissance critics in the analogies between rhetoric and poetry were not enough, there is Sidney's own view to encourage such an approach. Finally, the more common rhetorical figures organize his lyrics as completely as any other single device. But Renaissance rhetoric offers a view of style that pretends, for the modern reader at least, to be too inclusive, when in fact it reduces symbol and image to system and judges them almost entirely in terms of persuasive intent. For the modern critic the temptation to rely almost totally on this system is very great, but it means the acceptance of a bias that is too restricting. Sidney judges analogy or "similitude" as meant only to persuade "a willing hearer," but it is clear that to think of the poet as orator or rhetorician is to neglect his dramatic function. Again, Sidney damns certain types of ornate style on the grounds that they impede conviction and show off the writer as a poseur, but the imagery of his own ornate poems, although it may sometimes be superfluous or inhospitable to a rigorously thoughtful verse, nonetheless responds to a distinctive ordering of emotional experience. When we come to Sidney's plainer style, we find not only a drive towards greater intellectual clarity but also the beginnings of a dramatic expression in which the image, especially forms of personification, embodies action to represent states of mind. In the ordinary sense, a plain style may, as Sidney insists, be more persuasive, but that is not all we can legitimately expect and not all that style yields.

2.

Manner over Matter

*I*t is common to assume that the *Lady of May* poems, the translations of the *Psalms,* the *Arcadia* poems, *Astrophel and Stella,* and the miscellaneous pieces in *Certaine Sonets* follow a steady chronology of composition from 1578 to approximately 1583. Theodore Spencer's essay on Sidney's poetic development assumes that order and establishes an ascending hierarchy of quality upon it.[1] Unfortunately, the problem is not so neat. *The Lady of May* is easily dated because it was performed for a visit of the queen at Wanstead, the Earl of Leicester's castle, but William Ringler's investigations indicate that many of the *Arcadia* poems overlap and extend beyond the composition of *Astrophel and Stella,* and he is convinced that the translations of the *Psalms* should be dated in 1584. Finally, the poems in *Certaine Sonets* are of varying dates.[2] It is possible, therefore, that some of Spencer's

[1] "The Poetry of Sir Philip Sidney," *ELH,* XII (1945), 251–278.

[2] Ringler's findings are as yet unpublished, but he informs me that he dates the poems in *The Lady of May* in 1578; the "old" *Arcadia* poems, from late 1577 to late 1580, with all completed by the latter date except for a few revisions as late as 1584. He has "very strong evidence" for placing the composition of *Astrophel and Stella* in the summer of 1582. The ornateness of *The Lady of May* verses would suggest that Sidney's earlier verse is in that kind of style, but there is nothing to indicate that he abandoned it when he had reached a plainer, more perspicuous expression.

9

observations need to be modified, especially those leading to the view that all the poetry supposed to precede *Astrophel and Stella* is experimental prelude. There are, Spencer acknowledges, fine poems and evidence of technical maturity in the "early" pieces, but only in the sequence does Sidney's talent display itself with full assurance.

In reality, a much more profound difference separates *Astrophel and Stella* from the *Lady of May* poems, the *Psalms*, and the *Arcadia* poems. The latter three groups reflect a strong experimental spirit not found in the sequence, but it is more significant that this experimentation derives from a different creative principle. Furthermore, by no means all or even a majority of the *Arcadia* pieces betray the struggling apprentice or the green talent chiefly interested in technique at the expense of other things.

Those poems which are most striking for their ingenuity are scattered and, superficially at least, variable in type. Because they move beyond what is necessary for the conventional exercises of the novice, they are easily isolated, and we may wonder if they are uniformly the work of a novice at all. Occasionally Sidney appears anxious simply to master the intricacies of continental forms; occasionally, as in the *Psalms*, the effort is to work in a variety of stanza forms and line lengths; sometimes the impulse is towards rigidly consistent rhythm; at least once Sidney tries his hand at a game similar in motive to pattern and acrostic poems. It is here in his most eccentric poem that we can begin to observe the quest for symmetry underlying all the other forms of experiment:

> [1]Vertue, [2]beawtie, and [3]speach, did [1]strike, [2]wound, [3]charme,
> [1]My harte, [2]eyes, [3]eares, with [1]wonder, [2]love, [3]delight:
> [1]First, [2]second, [3]last, did [1]binde, [2]enforce, and [3]arme,
> [1]His workes, [2]showes, [3]suites, with [1]wit, [2]grace, and vow's [3]might.
>
> (*Works*, II, 53)

It is unnecessary to reprint the remaining lines to see that one must read by the numbers: "Vertue . . . did strike . . . my harte . . . with wonder," and so on. The piece only just deserves the name of poetry, but apart from its slight artistic value, it manages to make sense. We may note further that each line is split almost exactly in half by the

10

series of words, and this pattern extends through all fourteen lines. The result is monotonous symmetry indulged in for its own sake.

Sidney is never again so frivolous, but there are other poems in the *Arcadia* whose verbal tactics are quite as intricate. Consider, for example, the cluster of four poems near the beginning of Book 3. Each poem attempts to maintain one, two, or at the most three, rime sounds. One of the sonnets, "Since that the stormy rage of passions darcke," alternates "dark" and "light" as the rime words (a fairly common experiment).[3] The poem is not distinguished, but the necessity of maintaining the rime pushes Sidney to alter the sense of the two central images in repetition. There are also additional evidences of strong rhythmical pattern. Each quatrain is syntactically like the others, beginning with "since" and encompassing a subordinate clause, and, as in the last six lines, there is a profusion of word repetition:

> Since, as I say, both minde and sences darke
> Are hurt, not helpt, with piercing of the light:
> While that the light may shewe the horrors darke
> But cannot make resolved darkenes lighte:
>   I like this place, whereat the least the darke
>   May keepe my thoughtes, from thought of wonted light.
>   (*Works,* II, 8)

Another sonnet in the group has only one rime sound, and most of the lines contribute heavy alliteration and strong rhythmical balance to the already obvious pattern:

> My mangled mind huge horrors still doe fright,
> With sense possest, and claim'd by reasons right:
> Betwixt which two in me I have this fight,
> Wher who so wynns, I put my selfe to flight.
>   (*Works,* II, 9)

This may remind us of Dr. Johnson's remark about a woman's preaching, but the foremost organizing principle of these experiments deserves attention: they show an obvious, insistent pattern duplicated through several elements in the rhythm, as if Sidney's aim were to make all the resources of sound cooperate for a single balanced effect.

Exploring pattern in the same spirit but on a larger, more intricate

---

[3] See also *Astrophel and Stella,* Sonnet 89. Janet G. [Espiner-] Scott, *Les sonnets élisabéthains,* pp. 40–41, cites R. Fiorentino's "Deh non ritorni à rimenarne il giorno" as an example of the type.

scale, Sidney included two sestinas and a double sestina in the *Arcadia.* The latter, "You Gote-heard Gods," transcends technical exercise and will concern us in another context.[4] The sestinas, on the other hand, are a degree less ingenious and infinitely less accomplished. Their line-endings, which according to formula must not only be repeated but must also have a different order in each successive stanza, are all polysyllabic words concluding with a weak syllable, and Sidney takes pains to spread the monotonous, incessant beat by other means as well:

> Since wayling is a bud of causefull sorowe,
> Since sorow is the follower of evill fortune,
> Since no evill fortune equalls publique damage:
> Now Princes losse hath made our damage publique,
> Sorow, pay we to thee the rights of Nature,
> And inward griefe seale up with outward wailing.
>
> (*Works,* II, 138)

The list of the devices here is impressive. The first three lines commence with the same word (the rhetorical figure is anaphora)[5] and a periodic effect is managed through a carefully planned ordering of nouns, "wayling," "sorowe," "evill fortune," and "publique damage." In the next three lines these are arranged in reverse order. Further, the stanza is heavy with alliteration, assonance, consonance, and antithesis. The total effect is to highlight a strong rhythmical beat whose variations are muted. Needless to say, the discourse is obscure, but not through any great difficulty in the thought.

These examples outline the general directions of Sidney's experimental impulse. The tendency to hunt verbal ornament at the expense of other goals is plain, and so is the tendency for ornament to assume a more or less geometrical, balanced, and repeated shape. But whatever the deficiencies of such efforts, they are not eccentric for their times. Puttenham, in the remarks that follow, is merely the spokesman for much of the poetic bias of his age:

Then also must the whole tale (if it tende to perswasion) beare his iust and reasonable measure, being rather with the largest than with the scarcest. . . . Sweetenes of speech, sentence, and amplification, are therefore necessarie to an excellent Orator and Poet, ne may in no wise be spared from any of them.[6]

---

[4] See below, Chap. 3, pp. 44–47.

[5] Definitions of rhetorical figures are supplied in Appendix A.

[6] *The Arte of English Poesie,* pp. 197–198.

12

The notion of the poet as orator leads naturally to the view that for both of them the best expression is the "largest" and implies that an idea must have full and measured verbal clothing "if it tende to perswasion." Puttenham is simply echoing one of the more common biases of his times, and those who held to this opinion—Ascham was one of the most influential[7]—helped to point a large portion of English lyric, as well as prose, style towards a heightened embellishment. If one examines the verse of Spenser, of the miscellanies, and of the sonnet sequences of the nineties, it is clear that one of its more persistent characteristics is the extreme exploitation of the audible patterns of language. The impulse seems to be to give lyric a clear and balanced rhythmical shape beyond the requirements of imitation, and this impulse has some importance when we consider the attempts of a variety of poets—Dyer, Campion, Sidney, to name a few—to impose classical rhythms on English verse.

Quite recently John Buxton has written that Sidney's exclusive motive for classical experiments was to fit verse to the requirements of musical notation. He cites a passage from the *Arcadia*[8] which does not appear in any of its printed versions and comments: "Because of the quantitative effect of music when sung . . . Sidney, like de Baïf and his friends, thought it desirable to experiment with quantitative scansion on the Greek and Latin models."[9] Such experiments had been fashionable in France for some time. Du Bellay, Ronsard, and all the poets of the Pléiade had interested themselves in the musical performance of poetry, and Baïf in his *Académie de poésie et de musique* (1570) proposed detailed efforts to emulate in the vernacular the ancient identity of verse and music.[10] He and his colleagues toiled over quantitative verse to which musical notes could be adapted to match the metrical

[7] "Of Imitation," *Elizabethan Critical Essays*, ed. G. Gregory Smith (London, 1904), I, 6.

[8] The passage comes after the first eclogues; see *Works*, IV, 86. Buxton follows R. W. Zandvoort's inaccurate version (*Sidney's Arcadia, A Comparison of the Two Versions* [Amsterdam, 1929], pp. 11–12) which is drawn from the Queens College MS. of the *Arcadia*. Ringler's version is superior. See below, note 13.

[9] *Sir Philip Sidney and the English Renaissance* (London, 1954), p. 116.

[10] Frances A. Yates, *The French Academies of the Sixteenth Century* (London, 1947), pp. 36–42, provides a useful summary of this development. See her Appendix VIII for examples of the *vers mesurés* produced at Baïf's academy.

13

duration of the syllables. In England Campion was the most enthusiastic follower of this program, but as Catherine Ing demonstrates, he was successful only once.[11] There can be no doubt that Sidney was familiar with the French experiments or that he was aware of the widespread opinion that quantity was the common ground between the two arts of poetry and music. In the passage cited by Buxton[12] (a debate between two shepherds, Dicus and Lalus, as to the relative merits of "measured" and riming verse), Dicus, the exponent of quantitative verse, notes that words correspond to the "sounde" of music and measure to its "qualitie" in order that "for every sembref or minam it had his silable matched unto it, with a long foote or a short foote." The terminology is less than exact, but it is probable that "quality" means musical duration and "measure" syllabic duration, while the various components of the sound of words, volume, pitch, and pronunciation find their counterparts in melody and musical pitch. (Verse as read cannot imitate musical harmony; as sung by several voices it can, but this gets beyond the strictly rhythmic elements of language.) Unfortunately these remarks are not very illuminating. We cannot say that Dicus reflects Sidney's own views; the passage merely repeats a commonplace argument over the merits of two kinds of verse. Nor is it simply a question of assuming that when he wrote quantitative verse Sidney was largely concerned with exploring the musical properties of language. A good deal of his accentual verse is loosely designated as song. Nor is Sidney particular about what kind of music quantitative verse is especially adapted to. These uncertainties merely echo the general confusion of the age in its talk about the relations between poetry and music.[13]

Furthermore, the poems which Sidney wrote in imitation of classical forms are varied.[14] Two are in hexameters and are printed without

[11] *Elizabethan Lyrics* (London, 1951), p. 117–118.

[12] My excerpts are from the version printed by William Ringler from the St. John's College, Cambridge, MS. 308 (f. 40ᵛ), *PQ*, XXIX (1950), p. 72.

[13] See John Hollander, "The Music of Poetry," *Journal of Aesthetics and Art Criticism*, XV (1956), 232–244.

[14] James Applegate, "Sidney's Classical Meters," *MLN*, LXX (1955), 254–255, provides the following list:

Hexameters: "Lady reservd by the heav'ns to do pastors company honnor" (*Works*, II, 208; IV, 77).
"Faire rocks, goodly rivers, sweet woods, when shall I see peace? Peace" (I, 352; IV, 152).

any indication of the kind of music to be used in their performance. The same is true of his three Sapphics, and a song in the Aristophanic measure. In the absence of precise evidence one is at a loss to discuss their "musical" properties or propriety in any significant way. The same difficulty exists even when one attempts to evaluate their quantitative merits, for it is virtually impossible for an ear accustomed to the strong accentual basis of English rhythm to appreciate the duration of sound from syllable to syllable. We can roughly measure the relative duration of successive lines, but within the line we simply cannot eliminate the interference of speech stress. The only recourse is to see if the arrangement of stresses approximates the formal classical patterns.[15]

As an example the Sapphic concentrates on a form in which the rhythmical structure within the line is unbalanced, but the lines must,

---

Elegiac distichs: "Faire seeke not to be feard, most lovely beloved by thy servants" (IV, 307; *Certaine Sonets*).
"Fortune, Nature, Love, long have contended about me" (II, 208; IV, 75).
"Unto a caitife wretch, whom long affliction holdeth" (I, 357; IV, 318).
"Unto no body my woman saith she had rather a wife be" (II, 307; *Certaine Sonets*).

Sapphics: "If mine eyes can speake to doo harty errande" (I, 143).
"O my thoughtes, sweete foode my onely owner" (IV, 401). This is a rimed sapphic.
"Get hence foule griefe, the canker of the minde" (II, 50; IV, 214). Also a rimed sapphic.

Phalacean hendecasyllable: "Reason, tell me thy mind, if here be reason" (II, 236; IV, 156).

Asclepiadean: "O sweet woods the delight of solitarines" (II, 237; IV, 157).

Aristophanic: "When to my deadlie pleasure" (II, 316; *Certaine Sonets*).

Anacreontic: "My muse what ail's this ardour" (II, 234; IV, 155).

[15] An authoritative discussion of the theory behind these experiments is Gladys D. Willcock's "Passing Pitefull Hexameters," *MLR*, XXIX (1934), 1–19. She treats them as a serious and important effort to solve "the question of the interior structure of the line" (p. 1). As she remarks, there was much confusion before Puttenham (1589) because stress was not understood (although Sidney in the *Defence* [*Works*, III, 44] recognizes stress as fundamental to English rhythm), and she concludes that "when Elizabethans of this calibre [the allusion is to Webbe], and even of far better, talk about quantity and so on, they are speaking of something visible rather than audible" (p. 12). Yet Campion, when he attempted to adjust musical notation to the supposed quantity of the syllables in a poem, surely had audible duration in mind. See above note 12.

with minor variations, match each other, and the fourth line is always short.

$$
\begin{array}{l}
- \;u\; - \;- \;- \;u\;\; u\; - \;u\; - \;- \\
- \;u\; - \;- \;- \;u\;\; u\; - \;u\; - \;- \\
- \;u\; - \;- \;- \;u\;\; u\; - \;u\; - \;- \\
\qquad\qquad\quad - \;u\;\; u\; - \;-
\end{array}
$$

Here is a stanza from one of Sidney's Sapphics:

> If mine eyes can speake to doo harty errande,
> Or mine eyes language she doo hap to judge of,
> So that eyes message be of her received,
> > Hope we do live yet.
> > > (*Works*, I, 143)

Accentually, as well as quantitatively, the rhythm is almost impossible in the initial trochees if we try to make them adjust to the conventional pattern. Furthermore, the spelling of "doo" (perhaps not Sidney's responsibility, but it is the same in the version from the old *Arcadia*) when it should be a short or weak syllable is misleading, and it is scarcely easy to give the syllables of "errande," "judge of," or "re-ceaved" equal duration or stress. Read aloud so as to fit the Sapphic pattern, the lines would be eccentric indeed.

Yet Sidney has attempted some sort of order in the poem. For one thing, the short fourth line constitutes a varied refrain throughout. Another, and more important, device is rhetorical repetition. "Eyes" occupies the same position through three successive lines. And the first three lines have feminine endings. Thus, if Sidney has failed to produce an imitation of a perfect Sapphic, he has at least given his piece a certain rhythmical order. What emerges is verse with a very heavy beat, with at least five strong stresses to each long line and three to the short (here the classical pattern is successfully imitated). Furthermore, the stresses tend to emphasize the first half of each line, giving the latter half a falling rhythm. Prominence is given the expressive properties of the eyes, and they prepare rhythmically for the assertive weight of "Hope we do live yet."

Thus, whatever Sidney's intentions may have been (and, to repeat, we cannot be certain of these), there emerges a kind of symmetry encompassing the stanza, not the individual line, and it is a symmetry largely managed by standard rhetorical maneuver. If anything, Sidney overdoes the strong beat, and the same difficulty mars his two hexameter poems, "Faire rocks, goodly rivers, sweet woods, when shall I see

16

peace?" and "Lady reservd by the heav'ns to do pastors company honnor" (*Works*, I, 352; II, 208). The longer line and the general subjects of these pieces make them potentially more serious efforts. The first resolves itself into a lengthy lover's complaint which proceeds from point to point by means of an echo which twists the speaker's words by punning on them and continually turning his melancholy, idealistic worship of his mistress into a reproach of moral weakness. The echo device not only gives the verses a form of continuity, but also provides the major portion of whatever shape they have. And, since few of the lines seem to be true hexameters, Sidney once again depends upon the resources of formal rhetoric, this time to give the lines some internal organization in the midst of a general prosiness:

> O I doo know what guest I doo meete: it is *Echo*.   T'is *Echo*.
> Well mett *Echo*; aproch, and tell me thy will too.   I will too.
> (*Works*, I, 352)

The intent is to produce dialogue in which the speaker has the largest share and Echo the smallest, and the quality of the discourse hovers between the accents of casual speech and the monotonous regularity of the echo device. The concluding lines will serve to illustrate:

> Mockst thou those Diamonds, which onely be matcht by
>   the Godds?   Odds.
> Odds? what an odds is there, since them to the heav'ns I
>   preferre?   Erre.
> Tell yet againe, how name ye the goodly made evill?   A devill.
> Devill? in hell where such Devill is, to that hell I doo
>   goe.   Goe.
> (*Works,* I, 353)

The word repetition here differs from other examples we have seen in that it does not always serve to balance the line. In the second line above Sidney uses internal rime for balance, but it is offset by the strong pause after "Odds." Whatever consistency there is stems from the echo device and from the generally strong stress with which the lines begin. We discover, then, an experiment in which Sidney seems hesitant to embrace the consequences of fully casual discourse and seeks a corrective, however slight, not so much in the forms of classical metrics as in the repetitive properties of formal rhetoric.

The second hexameter poem, "Lady reservd by the heav'ns to do

17

pastors company honnor," is equally committed to a discursive procedure and moves even farther in its dependence on oratorical devices.
Zelmane, one of the two speakers (the poem is formally termed an
eclogue), emphasizes devotion to his mistress in lines approaching the
hyperbole of euphuism:

> First shall fertill grounds not yeeld increase of a good seed:
> First the rivers shall ceasse to repay their fludds to the *Occean*:
> First may a trusty Greyhounde transforme himselfe to a Tigre:
> First shall vertue be vice, and bewty be counted a blemishe,
> Ere that I leave with song of praise her praise to solemnize,
> Her praise, whence to the world all praise hath his only beginning.
>
> (*Works*, II, 210)

We are here brought back to Puttenham's "sweetenes of speech, sentence, and amplification" as the order of poetry, and these are not
reached by anything native to the classical hexameter. The noticeable
rhythm of the lines—and a rhythmical principle at various levels is
the most obvious motive for these experiments—may be traced directly
to Sidney's familiarity with the mechanics of formal rhetoric: in this
case, repetition within the line and through a group of lines, antithesis, and the period. Simply as attempts to get a kind of "music" out
of the relative duration of syllables, these pieces are meager accom-
plishments; as instances of a search for the means to adjust heightened
rhythmical patterns to various levels of discourse they hold more
interest.

The most successful of the classical poems is the song, "When to my
deadlie pleasure" (*Certaine Sonets*), composed in the Aristophanic
measure ($-\cup\cup-\cup--$). Once again the rhythmical structure
owes less to the classical form of the line than it does to rhetoric, but
for once Sidney is able to produce verses in which the stresses usually
coincide with the formal metrical pattern of the type:

> With violence of heav'nly
>
> Beautie tied, to vertue,
>
> Reason abasht retyred,
>
> Gladly my senses yeelded.[16]

[16] The horizontal dashes indicate quantitative pattern, the slanting lines,
stress.

18

The conflict in the first line (*vi-* must have a stress) may be deliberate; at least it effectively stresses an important word. And the extraordinary number of polysyllables crammed into so limited a space produces a strong insistent beat which gains interest from the feminine endings. As in the Sapphics, the effect is to enhance the importance of the early syllables in the line stressing the clipped quality of the short, blunt statements. But at the end of the poem Sidney reverts to the pattern of rhetorical monotony and overstatement:

> Thus may I not be from you:
> .Thus be my senses on you:
> Thus what I thinke is of you:
> Thus what I seeke is in you:
>   All what I am, it is you.

If the classical experiments remain formally uncertain, what can we say of their "musical" qualities? I would suggest that their "music" is not traceable to quantity any more than others of Sidney's poems are. The song above would be apt for performance by reason of its concentrated and continuous tempo, its symmetry of repetitious structure, and these are qualities we can discover again and again in short poems or songs which make no attempt to duplicate classical forms. Even in the perspective of burlesque Sidney's strategy is clear; it is merely heightened by the alliterative and assonantal symmetry of an "ill-noysed song":

> A Hatefull cure with hate to heale:
> A blooddy helpe with blood to save:
> A foolish thing with fooles to deale:
> Let him be bold that bobs will have.
>   (*Works*, I, 325)

A fitting complement to this extreme example of shaped and symmetrical rhythm is the *Lady of May* poems, which otherwise deserve little comment. There are three songs placed in a brief pastoral narrative, and they are probably Sidney's earliest surviving lyrics. Balanced and obvious repetition is their most prominent, indeed almost their only, distinguishing characteristic. The first, entitled "Supplication," is addressed to the Queen, and will stand for the others:

> To one whose state is raised over all,
> Whose face doth oft the bravest sort enchaunt,
> Whose mind is such, as wisest minds appall,

Who in one selfe these diverse gifts can plant;
How dare I wretch seeke there my woes to rest,
Where eares be burnt, eyes dazled, harts opprest?

Your state is great, your greatnesse is our shield,
Your face hurts oft, but still it doth delight,
Your mind is wise, your wisedome makes you mild,
Such planted gifts enrich even beggers sight:
So dare I wretch, my bashfull feare subdue,
And feede mine eares, mine eyes, my hart in you.
(*Works*, II, 330)

The awkward mixed metaphors, stale diction, and unrelieved metrical regularity betray Sidney's apprenticeship, but the fulsome enumeration of the details of praise and deliberate word repetition in a balanced line and through series of lines are typical of his later work.

Like these early pieces, Sidney's translations of the *Psalms* concentrate chiefly on verbal formality as a means of fixing the structure of the poem. Differences of opinion over the dating of the translations and Sidney's lack of choice of subject matter make them awkward to criticize. The act of translation is a species of submission. Sidney used the task to try his hand at a variety of verse forms, though no doubt his devotional interests were equally engaged. In any case, they reveal both his strengths and weaknesses as a technician and demonstrate the continuity of the particular kind of ornament to which he clings in most of the *Arcadia* verse.

For Theodore Spencer the *Psalms* show Sidney able to join extreme simplicity of diction and a clear metrical beat.[17] The observation is undeniable, for he preserves both elements through all the different line lengths and stanza forms he attempts. But at the same time he holds to his familiar strategy of a discourse primarily ordered by stylized rhetoric, and founded in the addition of like details to one another. Occasionally the more obvious rhetorical devices give way to a free concentration on stanzaic pattern and definite, even excessive, riming effects. In any case, Sidney's impulse is toward equivalence, and the total effect of the translations is seldom that of artlessness.

Much like the *Arcadia* poems, the variety in Sidney's version of the *Psalms* is in line and stanza form. Most often he uses a short line,

---

[17] "The Poetry of Sir Philip Sidney," *ELH*, XII (1945), 254–255.

tetrameter, trimeter, or occasionally dimeter. No single poem employs a two-beat line exclusively. A few are in rime-royal and terza rima, one or two in alexandrines, and all are iambic. Many of the poems have different line lengths set in a regular pattern of variation. Nevertheless, Spencer's remarks on the diction and rhythm and the tendency to stylistic symmetry point to an underlying consistency of esthetic purpose.

One reason for concluding that the *Psalms* chiefly interested Sidney as exercises in technique is his failure to suit formal variety to the specific content and mood of the individual pieces. Such adaptations would still be possible had he used one or two forms only through the entire forty-three poems he translated. On grounds of their content alone there seems to be little excuse for the switch from a six-line stanza with a seven-syllable line in Psalm XVI to a four-line stanza with couplets of ten and eight syllables in Psalm XVII. Both poems, pleas for security and justice, are very much alike. Furthermore, Sidney frequently struggles to maintain line length and rime with dubious success, as in

> Thy work it is such men safe in to hemm.
>
> (Psalm V, st. vii, l. 7)

The verses are also full of inversions, in spite of the obvious pursuit of simple, homely statement:

> Arise, ô Lord, in wrath thy self up sett.
>
> (Psalm VII, st. 6, l. 1)

At least once an insistent stanzaic pattern becomes a serious obstacle. There is an important change in the direction of thought in the following stanza, yet nothing in the meter or arrangement of the lines cooperates with this shift:

> Even multitudes be they
> That to my Soul do say
>   No help for you remaineth
> In God on whom you build
> Yet Lord thou art my shield
>   In thee my glory raigneth.
>
> (Psalm III, st. 2)

The text lacks punctuation, but even if it did not, the total effect of

21

the last three lines would be blurred, a muting of the contrast the Psalmist makes between the remarks of his enemies and his devotion to the Lord.

Elsewhere Sidney manages to confine sentence units strictly within stanzas or regular portions of stanzas. Even with allowances for a printer's alteration of text, the *Psalms* are ordinarily broken up into units containing entire statements: each stanza tends to be a complete and self-contained sentence. Such neatness also characterizes the sonnets in *Astrophel and Stella*, but the sequence is far more sophisticated in letting its style translate finer shadings of thought and emotion. Exactness in fitting the discourse to a preconceived lyric pattern appears to be one of the major experimental aims of the *Psalms*. Their identity with the sequence cannot be pursued too far.

In the realm of meter Sidney demonstrates a varying ability. Only one Psalm is completely regular (Psalm VIII), but in others the amount and purpose of the metrical variations fluctuates. In Psalm V the variations approach 25 per cent (nine variants in forty lines). Psalm VI has almost as high an incidence of irregularity (seven inversions in thirty-two lines), and here Sidney uses irregularity to good, if simple, effect. Compare the fifth and seventh stanzas:

> Loe I am tir'd while still I sigh and grone:
> My moistned bed proofes of my sorrow showeth:
> My bed (while I with black night moorn alone)
> With my teares floweth. . . .
> Gett hence you evill, who in my ill rejoice,
> In all whose works vainenesse is ever raigning:
> For God hath heard the weeping sobbing voice
> Of my complayning.

The fifth stanza is not entirely regular: there is a possible first-foot trochee in line one, and the third foot of line two is certainly inverted by the trochaic phrase. But the variations in the seventh stanza are far more strategic. "Evill" may or may not be elided; if not it syncopates the line. "Who in" is trochaic, and in the following line "vainenesse" and "raigning" intensify the suggestion of falling rhythm, which contrasts with and prepares for the triumphant, regular beat of "For God hath heard the weeping sobbing voice."

In a sense, this use of variation (it epitomizes Sidney's best results throughout the translations) is oratorical. It is a formal strategy, altering the rhythm not for colloquial effect, but to heighten the persuasiveness of shifts in meaning or alterations in tone. There is little attempt to imitate the fluctuations of spontaneous mental and emotional responses. Occasions where such a texture might be fashioned are rendered with deliberate formality:

> Then thinck I: Ah, what is this man:
>   Whom that greate God remember can?
>   And what the race of him descended,
>   It should be ought of God attended.
>
> (Psalm VIII, st. 4)

This level of ordered discourse is consistent with the character of the Psalms as rather stately expressions of man's relations with the Lord.

Another way in which Sidney relieves the strictness of his rhythms is occasional enjambment. In Psalm XVI it approaches the status of a consistent rule. At least it helps to soften the sing-song effect of the poem:

> For I know the deadly grave
>   On my soule noe pow'r shall have:
>   For I know thou wilt defend
>   Even the body of thine own
>   Deare beloved holy one,
>   From a fowle corrupting end.

These instances of departure from a strong, rather monotonous pattern are in no way remarkable in themselves. They are, perhaps, a reminder that Sidney is not committed merely to getting his accents and syllables in order, although this is clearly one of the main tasks of the translations.

Formally and in other ways the *Psalms* appear more primitive than the general run of poems in the *Arcadia*. As I have suggested, some of this difference stems from the frequently inept inversions, the excessive use of intensive verbs (adding "do" to the main verb is a distinct mannerism through all the poems), and a greater use of the short line with strong rimes. Formal rhetoric is less consistent in the *Psalms* than in the *Arcadia* poems, but when it does appear, Sidney, like an orator, uses it for a full and balanced pattern of emphasis. If the *Psalms* are not always to be identified by their symmetry, they are often capable of it. In Psalm XXII, which Sidney makes an echo of the tormented outcry of Christ on the cross, the opening stresses heavy word repetition in a balanced rhythmical frame:

> My God, my God, why hast thou me forsaken?
> Wo me, from me, why is thy presence taken?
> Soe farre from seeing, mine unhealthful eyes:
> So farre from hearing to my roaring cries.

> O God, my God, I crie while day appeareth:
> But God thy eare, my cryeng never heareth.
> O God the night, is privie to my plaint
> Yet to my plaint, thou hast no audience lent.

One of the most important things about such a style is the deliberate way in which it simplifies the elements of discourse. "God," "me," "seeing," "hearing," and their surrogate images occupy the prominent places in each line and are balanced in pairs. The verse focuses rhythmically and steadily on the motifs and simple emotions suggested by these terms and by their positions. They swirl around in a circle more intensely heightened as the word repetition and rhythmical pattern continue. The nature of the *Psalms* allows Sidney to go a certain distance with this style, but he does not have the freedom he enjoys in compositions entirely his own. In the latter, especially in the *Arcadia* and the *Certaine Sonets,* he is able to work with fully shaped poems. We have studied some examples of the most "experimental" (and perhaps the most tentative) of these, but, as I have suggested, the term may lose its value if it is used to describe all the pieces in which Sidney works with prominent and symmetrical orders of rhythm and rhetoric. In his songs we must begin to take Sidney more seriously because as we study them we shall begin to see that the formal symmetries he employs are not completely autonomous, although they may be redundant. In other words we shall begin to look at poems whose structures make sense in other terms, whose interest is not merely in the fulfillment of a technical plan.[18]

The songs discussed below are arranged in an order of increasing sophistication in their rhythm. No definite arrangement according to

[18] For a partial list of Sidney's songs which were given musical settings see Edmund H. Fellowes, *English Madrigal Verse, 1588–1632,* 2nd ed. (Oxford, 1947), index.

24

date of composition is feasible, although it may be that the best of them—those from the miscellaneous collection, *Certaine Sonets*—postdate the others. Generally Sidney is most impressive in songs using a varied line length, although some of his finest work appears in the songs in *Astrophel and Stella*, most of which are entirely regular. The majority of the *Arcadia* songs have a single line length and are patterned in restrictive, simple ways, much as the translations of the *Psalms*. But unlike the *Psalms* their rhythms are not so severely conditioned by the chosen stanza form or an obvious attempt to master consistency of meter. One of the simplest of these reduces its subject to a series of easy contrasts in a line that appears rigidly balanced:

> Wyth two strange fires of equall heate possest,
> The one of Love, the other Jealousie,
> Both still do worke, in neither finde I rest:
> For both, alas, their strengthes together tie:
> The one aloft doth holde, the other hie.
> > Love wakes the jealous eye least thence it moves:
> > The jealous eye, the more it lookes, it loves.
>
> These fires increase: in these I dayly burne:
> They feede on me, and with my wings do flie:
> My lovely joyes to dolefull ashes turne:
> Their flames mount up, my powers prostrate lie:
> They live in force, I quite consumed die.
> > One wonder yet farre passeth my conceate:
> > The fuell small: how be the fires so great?
> > > (*Works*, I, 310)

It is clear that the line, not the stanza, organizes the rhythm and provides a context for the pairs of opposing elements: love and jealousy, the fires and the self. In this fashion the poem moves forward, satisfying the order of contrast simply by repeating it, and the final couplet of the second stanza—in which Sidney attempts surprise by turning from what the speaker knows and can assert as fact to an unsolved paradox—fails to match the change in sense. Sidney preserves a regular meter when a departure might be in order. The usual cultivation of intensity through repetition outruns its usefulness.

Two brief songs, "Get hence foule Griefe, the canker of the minde" (*Works*, II, 50) and "The love which is imprinted in my soule," (*Works*, II, 55) are fashioned around a few key words or personifica-

25

tions. Here again the tendencies of the rhythm and subject matter coincide in evenly shaped discourse. The first disposes such items as grief, complaint, cares, sighs, tears, thought, and hope in the grammar of imperatives, and moves forward by an obvious plan:

> Get hence foule Griefe, the canker of the minde:
> Farewell Complaint, the misers only pleasure:
> Away vayne Cares, by which few men do finde
>   Their sought-for treasure.
> Ye helplesse Sighes, blowe out your breath to nought,
> Teares, drowne your selves, for woe (your cause) is wasted,
> Thought, thinke to ende, too long the frute of thought
>   My minde hath tasted.

The last two stanzas complement these by welcoming the images of complaint transformed into joy. As before Sidney's chief concern is to fit his subject to a measurable pattern, to see it and express it in the geometry of completed form, although the rhythm has its judicious departures in slightly altered pauses and an inversion or two, and his habit of alternating feminine and masculine rimes (one of his more persistent devices in short lyrics) makes a pattern of light contrast between successive lines. There is even a kind of animation to the song, a vitality lacking in the translations of the *Psalms* and other labored exercises.

Of the longer "musical" pieces, the sestinas, a hymn or two, and some forcefully cadenced pastoral singing contests, as well as the songs in *Astrophel and Stella*, something will be said in later chapters. On the level of rhythm these display the same impulses we are discussing here. And if we are to judge by these, Sidney's effort to produce the rounded, obtrusive lyric structure is plain. The ornament of the poem appears to be both skeleton and flesh. Order of all kinds, of syntax, rhythm, image, coincides on one level of symmetrical proportions, and in this respect Sidney's verse is the climax of a generation of poetic endeavor to control the tempo and the contours of lyric expression and to seek intensity through repetition and overstatement. *Tottel's Miscellany* is early evidence of these directions (one slipshod poem uses anaphora through thirty lines[19]), and the verse of Googe and

[19] *Tottel's Miscellany*, No. 251; ed. Hyder E. Rollins, 2 vols. (Cambridge, Massachusetts, 1928), I, 196.

Gascoigne,[20] different in other ways and often simple and direct, is nevertheless committed to severely shaped and amplified style. Judged by his lesser work Sidney has merely succeeded in polishing the devices of his forerunners.

But even in his songs he occasionally reaches a more sophisticated concept of structure. One or two of these, in *Certaine Sonets*, are among the best the Elizabethans could produce and may serve to demonstrate what can be accomplished within the restrictions of verse produced to be sung, verse ostensibly committed to heavy verbal ornament. In these songs the subject remains simple, intellectually undeveloped, but the centers of interest are not therefore wholly in ornament. The framework of "Ring out your belles, let mourning shewes be spread" severely limits the range of the discourse, but the structure is subtly and quietly varied:

> Ring out your belles, let mourning shewes be spread,
>   For love is dead:
>   All Love is dead, infected
>   With plague of deepe disdaine:
>   Worth as nought worth rejected,
>   And Faith faire scorne doth gaine.
>   From so ungratefull fancie,
>   From such a femall franzie,
>   From them that use men thus,
>   Good Lorde deliver us.

(Certaine Sonets)

The form is the same through all four stanzas, with the final quatrain serving as a refrain. Bruce Pattison's remarks about the influence of musical considerations on the poet surely apply here, for the refrain, the obvious narrowness of the idea, the easy and graceful alliteration, all maintain the steady incantatory rhythm needed for the litany.[21] These qualities are familiar in poems whose sole task seems to be to present proportionate, repeated, and predictable form. But in other ways "Ring out your belles" is neither commonplace nor banal.

It has both local and extended balance: the meter of each line varies

---

[20] The most extreme example from Googe is "The oftener sene, the more I lust," *Eglogs, Epytaphes, & Sonettes* (1563), ed. Edward Arber (London, 1871), p. 96. Gascoigne's "The Steele Glasse" makes liberal use of the device.

[21] *Music and Poetry of the English Renaissance* (London, 1948), p. 141 and esp. pp. 150–155.

internally, but the pattern of one line may be repeated in another. Although lines one and two differ radically, their forms are repeated at the opening of the succeeding stanzas. But the variations are still important. They offer us hints of what Sidney was able to accomplish on a more extended and versatile scale in the sonnets, and they demonstrate his ability to use rhythmic form, however lightly, to beckon our attention away from its self-contained, circular, balanced shape even as it retains these qualities.

The first line itself is a warning that Sidney has modified his rather strained devotion to the neatly balanced line. The opening phrase, "Ring out your belles," probably calls for four strong, nearly equal stresses, although it might be construed as iambic, in which case there would be a sharp conflict between meter and spoken stress. The remainder of the line is more surely iambic. This colliding rhythm gives way to two simple iambs in the short second line, while the third line adds a foot and an initial spondee (or hovering accent: "love" demands more emphasis than the ordinary weak syllable by virtue of its position equivalent to "love" in the line before). What Sidney manages here is the apparently effortless task of a slight but very important shift in speech emphasis in two lines which superficially amount to nothing more than a commonplace rhetorical recurrence. In the fourth line Sidney reverts to consistent iambic structure, but the fifth opens with a trochee, possibly two, and has a weak final syllable. Probably the sixth line should be scanned iambically, but "faire" needs a strong spoken stress. This group of lines, regarded in isolation, is not only radically irregular in meter, but the irregularities are deliberate and effective. It is obvious that the verse aims at facilitating musical performance through its use of heavy stress, announcing to composer, musician, and vocalist alike the areas where their emphases should fall. Less obvious, perhaps, is the particular suitability of this small group of lines for reading aloud, for exclusively poetic performance. In the experiments we have considered previously Sidney's concern for the performing voice is always self-consciously oratorical, always intent on satisfying a concept of verbal shape, to which other matters may be sacrificed. In "Ring out your belles" we still have a strong and unmistakable verbal shape built on a principle of recurrence, but we have as well a metrical and vocal rhythm following the demands of *changing* emphasis in mood and subject matter.

28

The first line is emotionally strong, mingling insistence with mournfulness, after which the blunt statement of the second line is almost shocking; the change of rhythms is appropriate to the shift, as is the extreme contrast between the long and short lines. With the third line the emotion gets a second breath and proceeds to elaborate the discovery that love is dead; the second line had uttered this discovery with deceptive finality. The accent on "All" is necessary for the recovery of strength which is not fully apparent until we know that this line not only is longer than its predecessor but leads to enjambment as well. Emphasis in the fourth line comes through a different medium, the alliterated phrase "deepe disdaine," while in the fifth line the repetition of "worth" and the surprising accents offer still another approach. In the sixth line Sidney uses rhythmical counterpoint, alliteration, and assonance to assist the change to irony. Finally, the refrain, set off from the rest by heightened repetition (anaphora), has three rhythmically equivalent lines. A differently keyed emotion, approaching the litany, needs to be preserved unchanged, whereas the first six lines call for an accompaniment to subtle changes in feeling.

In moving from Sidney's merely "experimental" verse to such a poem as this, we move from poetry with all the signs of technical struggle and obvious effects to poetry which he is able to control on his own terms, but we do not change from ornamented to plain discourse. The emotion of "Ring out your belles" is public, formal, and impersonal. Its voice is flexible but scarcely spontaneous, even in appearance. Nor, it should be repeated, have we necessarily encountered an older or more practiced Sidney: we can only conclude that moments of ingenuity occasionally yield to fully conceived and executed poems. "Ring out your belles" may be of late composition, but it is probably no later than several others founded in rather clear and rigid structural proportion. We must remember, too, that in spite of the delicate rhythmical modifications in this song, it is like its less accomplished companion pieces in keeping to a strong, monotonous, overemphatic beat, which elsewhere Sidney employs with less discrimination. He is still rendering experience ceremonially, even effusively; and he conceives and executes it in terms of a symmetry which stamps almost all his verse except *Astrophel and Stella*.

3.

Ornate Structure and Imitation

*T*he geometry of Sidney's verse, its strong and often excessive sense of proportion, is more than a matter of rhythm and more than a tendency to balance. Many of the shorter poems we have examined pursue a circular course, and some of the longer ones seem headed in this direction, but the patterns of rhetoric include something besides repetition. Whether the figures are periodic or schemes of amplification, they are likely to distend and swell poetic statement. Thus, added to the symmetrical conception of Sidney's *Arcadia* poems, is another principle which we may examine from several angles. Amplification, one of the central features in Puttenham's description of a proper style, is often equivalent to overstatement, and it encourages delay in the completion of meaning. It may mean, also, the duplication of imagery, a piling of trope on trope in addition to the heaping of words and their statements within an obvious rhythmic pattern. Generally, such a method may be called Ciceronian, in so far as it satisfies the stylistic objectives described by Cicero for an ample style,[1] or fulfills the re-

[1] *Orator* (Loeb Classical Library: London and Cambridge, Massachusetts, 1952), sects. 97–99: "The orator of the third style is magnificent, opulent, stately and ornate; he undoubtedly has the greatest power." Bishop Hall refers to Sidney's "high-stil'd *Arcady*" (cited by G. Gregory Smith, *Elizabethan Critical Essays*, I, 402). More precise details of what Cicero understands by the

30

quirements of Puttenham that the figures "passe the ordinary limits to common utterance, and be occupied of purpose to deceive the eare and also the minde, drawing it from plainnesse and simplicitie, to a certaine doublenesse."[2]

Puttenham has in mind, not the coexistence of different levels of meaning, but the complication of discourse by extending it, by including more than is necessary for the simple requirements of plain meaning, by making a statement twice, presenting it in its most formal guise. The implications of Sidney's use of amplified style go past the limits of rhetorical formality, or at least past the commoner figures. This rhetoric is simply part of a general exploration in formal procedures of many kinds, for in certain of his poems narrative description and personification assist the figures in encouraging an extended formality. Finally, we shall discover behind this formality not just a fondness for the orator's overemphasis but a mimetic principle which shapes the style according to a definite attitude towards human experience. Much has been said of the Elizabethans' lush and exuberant style as a kind of childlike fascination for words, an impulse which gives the literature of the period its extraordinary vitality but burdens it with looseness and imprecision. In Sidney's case the charge is not true. His language is rarely loose, in diction or form, and never without a shaping principle behind it.

There are several common figures of amplification which Sidney employs—*the collectour, epanados, hirmus, prolepsis, merismus, synathroesmus,* and *asyndeton* are the most prominent[3]—but the ugly jargon of the terms is less important than the effects they produce at Sidney's hands. Delay is the most noticeable of these effects, and it may be continued through an entire poem:

> Since so mine eyes are subject to your sight,
> That in your sight they fixed have my braine;
> Since so my harte is filled with that light,
> That onely light doth all my life maintaine;

---

grand style may be inferred from his list of devices to be avoided or modified in the plain style. See below, Chap. 5. Cicero's purpose here is largely descriptive; he should not be held responsible for the excesses of his Renaissance admirers, the Ciceronians.

[2] *The Arte of English Poesie*, p. 154.

[3] Definitions of these and other figures important to Sidney's style may be found in Appendix A.

> Since in sweete you all goods so richly raigne,
> That where you are no wished good can want;
> Since so your living image lives in me,
> That in my selfe your selfe true love doth plant;
> > How can you him unworthy then decree,
> > In whose chiefe parte your worthes implanted be?
> > > (*Works*, I, 155)

These lines are syntactically shaped into parallel clauses, while hirmus, the main rhetorical figure, accomplishes its task of adding element to element before the sense of the poem is finally brought to completion. Balanced recurrence, combining with and furthering the strategy of delay, stresses anticipation of the climax. The mind of the reader is led on by frustration as well as symmetry. Yet in spite of such counterpoint the poem lacks any dramatic development, and its all too obvious formality finds relief only in the simplicity of the wording in the final couplet. It is worth observing that here Sidney eases the word repetition characteristic of the earlier lines.

Another form of amplification, the collectour, tends to draw together details already elaborated and unmistakable in meaning, but it does so only after avoiding a quick and simple resolution of idea.

> Over these brookes trusting to ease mine eyes,
> (Mine eyes even great in labour with their teares)
> I layde my face; my face wherein there lyes
> Clusters of clowdes, which no Sunne ever cleares.
> > In watry glasse my watrie eyes I see:
> > Sorrowes ill easde, where sorrowes painted be.
>
> My thoughts imprisonde in my secreat woes,
> With flamie breathes doo issue oft in sound:
> The sound to this strange aier no sooner goes,
> But that it dooth with *Echoes* force rebound.
> > And make me heare the plaints I would refraine:
> > Thus outward helps my inward griefes maintaine.
>
> Now in this sande I would discharge my minde,
> And cast from me part of my burdnous cares:
> But in the sand my tales foretolde I finde,
> And see therein how well the writer fares.
> > Since streame, aier, sand, mine eyes and eares conspire:
> > What hope to quench, where each thing blowes the fire?
> > > (*Works*, I, 257)

Several figures participate in the discourse,[4] but the collectour dominates the rest, wrapping up each important image in one line: "Since
streame, aier, sand, mine eyes and eares conspire." The statement
offers nothing new; it merely demonstrates the unity and contour of
what has been said before.

But if the rhetoric of amplification merely attempts to announce the
shape and overstate the force of the ideas, it also gives Sidney the
leisure to explore these ideas, however commonplace their presentation.
The verses above nourish the seeds of a developing, moving subject
whose modest interest lies in the discovery of the speaker that his
complaints are futile. Another mode of beginning which attempts
to frame a mild complexity by rhetorical expansion occurs in the double
sestina, "You Gote-heard Gods."

> For she, whose parts maintainde a perfect musique,
>> Whose beautie shin'de more then the blushing morning,
>> Who much did passe in state the stately mountaines,
>> In straightnes past the Cedars of the forrests,
>> Hath cast me wretch into eternal evening,
>> By taking her two Sunnes from these darke vallies.
>>> (*Works*, I, 142)

In this stanza conclusiveness is briefly frustrated by a series of clauses.
The figure, a modified form of synathroesmus,[5] combines interruption
of the main clause, fullness in the rhythm, and effusive feeling. The
strategy of suspense allows Sidney time to introduce an idea corollary
to the oblique statement of the lady's absence, that of her harmonious
and stately beauty. Together the two justify the quality of emotion,
admiration and regret, and suggest their blending. The rhetorical
form with its twin rhythmical motifs—local balance and periodicity—
seems fitting. Yet a form useful for handling some degree of complication, as this example demonstrates, may be psychologically and intellectually static. Movement is paralyzed so that the lady's beauty may

---

[4] Anadiplosis (the repetition of "mine eyes" in lines one and two); epizeuxis
("my face; my face" in line three); ploce (the recurrence of "watry" and "sor-
rowes" in lines five and six); epanados (governing the syntax of the first two
stanzas). These figures ensure proportion locally within the line and extend
it over the whole range of the poem, giving it the appearance of a rigid, overemphatic structure.

[5] See Appendix A.

33

be attested four times. The technique works to arrest and expand, not advance, the discourse.

What we have discovered in these examples, in the midst of a rhetorical formalism that is entirely standard and entirely within an ornate poetic tradition, is an attempt to use style mimetically, although on a thoroughly stylized level. We cannot assume that Sidney discerned a form in the idea itself and let it dictate his style; the view of frustrated love he works with the form he chooses are too obviously conventional to permit us to erect such a hierarchy of intentions, although when we examine the double sestina in its entirety we shall see that Sidney was particularly fortunate in bringing the two together. At any rate, it is now evident on a small scale that Sidney is interested in more than ornament, however experimental, however self-conscious decorative the verse may seem.

It is commonly assumed that Renaissance artists and critics accepted a fundamentally Aristotelian view of imitation: the representing of general truths in nature. Their copying never deliberately sought verisimilitude of the kind we expect today, an image related to nature as waxed fruit mirrors the reality. They tried rather to capture the significance of the external world of object and action. As Sidney remarks, art makes its own order, "an other nature,"[6] and whatever photographic realism might be found in a poem would be incidental. Yet the transformed order of art is not easy to demonstrate on the level of style if we wish to decide precisely in what way that order is mimetic. And ornamental style of the kind we are treating here may seem to be merely schematic, or at best imitative of other orders of style. Sometimes, and this is usually true of Spenser, the shapes of style may further symbolism and allegory. Finally, ornamental verse tends to submit to the requirements of oratorical persuasion, highlighting one thought and shadowing another for the sake of emphasis. At this point we may have to be content with a definition of mimesis which simply refers to the rendering of universal truth, abstract or concrete.

But when we recall that some of Sidney's most ornamental verse

---

[6] *The Defence of Poesie* (*Works*, III, 8). Sidney adds that the center of the work of art lies in its "*Idea*, or fore conceit," from which follows his definition of imitation as a "speaking *Picture*" (the same, III, 9) or "that faining notable images of vertues, vices, or what els" (the same, III, 11).

seems disposed to ornament for its own sake, and when we find that rather different poetic subjects get the same stylistic treatment, we may conclude either that he applied his rhythm and rhetoric without much discrimination or that the question of imitation is simply irrelevant. The first possibility is occasionally true: there are poems in which ornate rhythms and rhetoric are pursued with a relentless and crude monotony as if the style were little more than habit. But in other poems, equally committed to symmetry, amplitude, and repetition, Sidney achieves a more judicious and functional use of ornament. In the general question of the suitability of highly formal style, the problem of mimesis is not beside the point. Sidney preserves his stylistic system but adjusts it more clearly and certainly to an idea. Whether style imitates or creates the shape and particular quality of an idea is possibly unanswerable if we believe that ideas are known to us only in their verbal clothing, but in certain poems the subject comes to Sidney already shaped by tradition, and it is the aptness of his copy which must be examined.

The most obvious and familiar of his poems based on a traditionally fashioned concept is "My true love hath my hart, and I have his." It centers in the notion that the souls of lovers are united by an exchange, and the notion of transference immediately suggests a contour easily rendered by the style:

> My true love hath my hart, and I have his,
> By just exchange, one for the other giv'ne.
> I holde his deare, and myne he cannot misse:
> There never was a better bargaine driv'ne.
> His hart in me, keepes me and him in one,
> My hart in him, his thoughtes and senses guides:
> He loves my hart, for once it was his owne:
> I cherish his, because in me it bides.
> His hart his wound receaved from my sight:
> My hart was wounded, with his wounded hart,
> For as from me, on him his hurt did light,
> So still me thought in me his hurt did smart:
> > Both equall hurt, in this change sought our blisse:
> > My true love hath my hart and I have his.
> > > (*Works*, II, 17)

None of the stylistic elements we have noticed for other ornamental

35

poems is missing here. Except in the first and last lines, the pauses come after the second foot; the halves of most of the lines also match each other in syntax. This pattern works so that the rhythm within the line coincides with the alternation of statement between the two actors of the poem and is repeated from line to line with only minor changes. The familiar strategy of symmetrical balance organizes the tempo, and further evidence for a geometrical form appears in the beginnings of the first two lines of the second and third quatrains: "His hart . . . My hart." Finally, in addition to the matched pronouns, "his" and "my," which occur everywhere, there is a duplication of rhetorical formula, as in lines nine and ten with their play on "wound," and the entire sonnet rounds into a structural whole by the recurrence of the first line as the last. The effect is one of congruity, all the levels of style echoing each other and joining to match and illustrate the quality of the lovers' identity.

This kind of imitation is basically very simple, for the traditional notion of interchange of souls carries with it a formal arrangement which Sidney was able to borrow. Furthermore, that arrangement exactly suits his habits of balanced and amplified style. Rhythm, syntax, and rhetoric are used in exactly the same ways we have seen in the experimental poems, but here there is no sense that the subject matter has been artificially tailored to satisfy the needs of ornament. On the contrary, rhythmical repetition and amplitude of statement bring out qualities inherent in the idea. Imitation becomes a process of reflecting something and giving it polished and added stress.

In the realm of imagery the question of imitation becomes more complicated. But, as in the uses of ornament we have already seen, Sidney's maneuvers with imagery seem designed for uniform effects. In the *Arcadia* poems there is rarely any use in looking for imagery fashioned to imitate states of mind or mental or psychological processes. Just as the movement of "My true love hath my hart, and I have his" is circular and ultimately static, so the imagery of the *Arcadia* usually fixes and embellishes emotions, narrowing and concentrating its effects. This is especially true of the blazon, perhaps the simplest of conventional devices. Ordinarily it is convenient for praise and offers the poet a ready-made frame for his portrait. And, of course, the blazon is the most obvious sort of imitation. Sidney uses

36

it eleven times (five times in *Astrophel and Stella*).[7] The most extended is called "a Songe the Shepeheard *Philisides* had . . . sunge of the beutyes of his unkynde Mistris":[8]

> What Toungue can her perfections tell?
> In whose eche parte all penñs may dwell.
> Her hayre fyne Laces made of golde,
> In Curled knottes Mans thoughte to holde,
> But that her forehead sayes in mee,
> A whiter Bewty yow may see,
> Whiter in deede, more white then snowe,
> Which on Colde wynters face dothe grow.
>
> (*Works*, IV, 223)

The catalogue moves from head to foot and back again, comparing each of the lady's features to various objects of value or beauty. The technique is rather pedestrian, and Sidney occasionally descends to the ridiculous: "Her Nose and Chynñ suche Ivory weares, / No *Elephant* so perfect beares." Also, the variety of the images is superficial; their real significance lies in their function as details reiterating and overemphasizing the lady's supreme worth. And, inevitably, the obvious formalism of the blazon mirrors its subject only at a distance. The pretended immediacy of the list of physical features is drained of all life and movement. The portrait is frozen and deliberately remote, suggesting perhaps the inaccessibility of the chaste mistress.

But however contrived such a technique may be, it is a valid kind of imitation in the Renaissance understanding of the word. As Sidney uses it here the blazon is meant not as a photograph of the living presence of a woman but as an image of her significance. Secondarily, perhaps, it represents the attitude of the speaker who contemplates that significance, but Sidney does not develop this motif very far. Donne's famous blazon, "Loves Progress," is more advanced in that its real point is the shifting and complicated mental and emotional reactions of the lover. But the organizing principle is still very simple. The poet need only catalogue human features in their conventional

---

[7] See Appendix B.

[8] The poem also appears in the revised *Arcadia* (*Works*, I, 218), but the older version is reprinted here for the sake of its prose introduction. The differences between the two versions are largely in the spelling.

order, and he has at command an easy method of amplification. All the images illustrate "her perfection."

Yet swollen discourse need not be so elementary. The deliberate lack of conciseness often found in the *Arcadia* verse may be there to dress out some particular quality of feeling or mood, and Sidney is quite capable of letting his images gather emotional energy simply through wordiness. Consider the leisurely movement with which the following poem begins:

> Now was our heav'nly vaulte deprived of the light
> With Sunnes depart: and now the darkenes of the night
> Did light those beamye stars which greater light did darke:
> Now each thing that enjoy'd that firie quickning sparke
> (Which life is cald) were mov'd their spirits to repose,
> And wanting use of eyes their eyes began to close:
> A silence sweet each where with one consent embraste
> (A musique sweet to one in carefull musing plaste)
> And mother Earth, now clad in mourning weeds, did breath
> A dull desire to kisse the image of our death:
> When I, disgraced wretch, not wretched then, did give
> My senses such reliefe, as they which quiet live,
> Whose braines broile not in woes, nor breast with beatings ake,
> With natures praise are wont in safest home to take.

> > (*Works*, I, 394–395)

This is clearly the prelude to a fairly long poem, in effect a dream vision for which the evocation of the slow and sweet approach of evening is apt. The alexandrine also permits Sidney time to build up the mood gradually and completely. Such an opening is indeed decorative and ornate; in some ways it is reminiscent of the long preambles to medieval dream visions. And yet in all these lines very little is said. The narrator, to reduce his statements to their essentials, merely announces that he was preparing himself for a quiet sleep at sundown, noting parenthetically that when this happened he was not wretched, as he is now at the time of his narration. Yet he spends thirteen lines on his preliminary report, noting the obvious and irrelevant facts that light goes from the world at dusk, that the light of the stars, which had been hidden by the sun, then appears, that all living things approach sleep at this hour, and that silence follows. It is hard to imagine a less efficient beginning even for a narrative poem, and yet it would be wrong to conclude that what happens in these lines is unimportant or that Sidney's use of imagery is "inorganic." Decorative or ornate detail has a legitimate purpose, bearing a load of associative meanings necessary to the quality of the poem yet not centrally concerned with urging its meaning forward.

Perhaps the significance of this deliberately verbose style will be clearer if examined in a sonnet, where the poet is necessarily more restrained in making his point. The subject matter is reminiscent of the *Arcadia* poem.

> When far spent night perswades each mortall eye,
>   To whom nor art nor nature graunteth light,
>   To lay his then marke wanting shafts of sight,
>   Clos'd with their quivers in sleeps armory;
>
> With windowes ope then most my mind doth lie,
>   Viewing the shape of darknesse and delight,
>   Takes in that sad hue, which with th' inward night,
>   Of his mazde powers keepes perfit harmony:
>
> But when birds charme, and that sweete aire, which is
>   Mornes messenger, with rose enameld skies
>   Cals each wight to salute the floure of blisse;
>
> In tombe of lids then buried are mine eyes,
>   Forst by their Lord, who is asham'd to find
>   Such light in sense, with such a darkned mind.
>   (*Astrophel and Stella,* Sonnet 99)

To some extent the metaphorical complication of this sonnet—Sidney transfers the natural images to Astrophel's state of mind very abruptly —defines one difference between *Astrophel and Stella* and the *Arcadia* poems. Intellectually the verse of the sequence moves in more directions in a shorter space of words, and is therefore usually more economical. But the example just quoted nevertheless fits the standards of ornateness I am concerned with. Sidney could state the proposition about the links between Astrophel's state of mind and the general qualities of night and morning more briefly and with less conscious formality, yet he prefers tactics of indirection: we do not need to know that there is no light to see by in the dead of night or that the absence of light makes the eyes close. Nor do we need to be told that birds sing in the morning and the light is rose-colored, but we do require the facts that birds "charme," that the air is "sweete," and that there is something blissful about the time of day. Such overtones of feeling are essential as a contrast to the "darkned mind" of the speaker, Astrophel. This is an elaborate structure for surprise or emphasis, and formally it resembles the periodic figures of rhetoric. Secondary details thrown in our way and added to each other, reiterate the obvious much as a drum strikes the same note again and again. We are offered a full diet of descriptive images before we get to the main course.

Indirection and delay through the use of imagery are a type of imitative form useful in arranging details for particularly heavy concentration. The surface tone of poems constructed on this principle is usually homogeneous, or if it changes, the shift is pointed, deliberate, and stylized. It is not a kind of imitation which mirrors the spontaneous movement of thought or emotion, but it does seem designed to render and highlight fixed qualities of feeling in their strongest colors. The speaker's emotion may accord or contrast with the world around him; in either case, the images are managed to make emotion and its natural context unequivocal.

Personification is the most stylized kind of imitation, although it may well serve a dramatic purpose, as it does in *Astrophel and Stella*. In the *Arcadia* verse, however, we are more aware of the conscious distortion of reality, and personification here is crucial to the structure of Sidney's ornateness. Thirty-seven of the *Arcadia* poems have it as an important formal device,[9] and its influence over the conduct of the imagery takes three directions. First, it provides a logical center for kinds of images; in other words a personified feeling or object may be a focus for imagery. Second, it encourages obliquity of discourse, for although personification may be a living vessel for speech, it tends to remove attention from the main subject of the verse. When one of Sidney's characters addresses a tree or a brook on the topic of love, we are aware of them as more than parts of the natural setting. When Sidney praises a lady by personifying her eyes, they and not the lady occupy the foreground of attention, and they may provoke the appearance of other images, such as sun, stars, or light, drawing us still further away from the lady herself. Third, personification releases the feelings, allowing their full expression and pushing them outward to mingle with the natural world.

[9] See Appendix C.

40

These three aims may unite in one poem, or they may live singly. Personification used to control and direct imagery is a simple, easily understood function. For example, in *"Phaebus* farewell, a sweeter Saint I serve," each stanza opens with the same form of address, and the personification stands at the very center of the idea. The speaker switches his semi-religious allegiance from Apollo to his mistress, and the associated images work a neat contrast between the two, as in the second stanza:

> *Phaebus* farewell, a sweeter Saint I serve.
> Thou art farre off, thy kingdome is above:
> She heav'n on earth with beauties doth preserve.
> Thy beames I like, but her cleare rayes I love:
> Thy force I feare, her force I still do prove.
> (Works, II, 5)

Like most amplified discourse, this is hyperbole in the guise of logical definition, or perhaps it would be better to say that the discourse is a combination of both: the distinctions between the effects of "service" to the two deities, which define emotional attitudes, are the bases of high praise. Furthermore, Sidney has no need to strain the images to make them suitable to the personification of the sun. Tradition, of course, counts for a good deal: Phoebus is a god and so needs a kingdom; he is the sun and has forceful beams, and so on. These links occur automatically and smoothly. The personification is clearly useful to focus the rhythmical pattern and arrange the images. A more elaborate instance of this form of control may be seen in the sestina "Farewell ô Sunn, *Arcadias* clearest light" (*Works*, II, 143–144). Its first stanza repeats the address to the sun in every line, and the entire poem celebrates the benefits of the sun to man through a series of secondary images—color, preciousness, light as joy, light as wisdom—all placed in different order in different stanzas. Such patterning is in danger of removing the verse at too great a distance from anything we may consider real and thus losing all imitative value, but it can usually be justified on the grounds that it gives human emotion a significant, if ritualistic, relation to the natural world or to the world of ideas. The greater verisimilitude of the plain style is absent here.

The second category of personification, in which the device symbolizes something else indirectly, always seems contrived. In "Swete glove the swetenes of my secrett blisse" (*Works*, II, 239) the glove is merely an excuse for conceited praise, a proxy for its wearer, and the poem becomes an exercise in ingenious imagery set in a patterned context ("Swete glove the swete despoyles of sweteste hande, / Fayer hand the fayreste pledge of fayrer harte"). The following, from *Astrophel and Stella*, is more skilful:

> O eyes, which do the Spheares of beautie move,
>> Whose beames be joyes, whose joyes all vertues be,
>> Who while they make *Love* conquer, conquer *Love*,
>> The schooles where *Venus* hath learn'd Chastitie.
>
> O eyes, where humble lookes most glorious prove,
>> Only lov'd Tyrants, just in cruelty,
>> Do not, ô do not from poore me remove,
>> Keepe stil my *Zenith*, ever shine on me.
>> (Sonnet 42)

Justification for the address is furnished by the commonplace notion that the eyes, both in love and in other kinds of experience, are the most important of the senses, the means through which the intelligence and the passions can react to what happens outside the self; thus they had a special value for the Petrarchan lover, and conceits based on them are far from rare.[10] Here, the background of convention makes the role of the eyes as symbolic of the lady herself perfectly normal, even though Sidney adds a number of disparate images. It is worth mentioning, also, that the links between these images are extremely tenuous (for instance, "conquer" and "schooles" seem far apart, and the reader is perhaps meant to supply the concept of authority to relate them); a form of logical ellipsis appears to be at work, lending the poem something of a "metaphysical" flavor. More obviously, however, the form of the discourse is based on a series of epithets describing the lady herself, overstating her beauty, chastity, and humility, with definition of the meaning and effects of these qualities a complicating factor.

Once again we have the sort of imitation which derives the significance of the subject through its images, and once again it is an imitation which is not dramatic or even prone to copy the spontaneous movement of the mind or feelings of the speaker. On the other hand, the

---

[10] There is an extensive list of their occurrence in Lisle C. John's *The Elizabethan Sonnet Sequences*, pp. 195–200.

speaker's voice governs the quality of mimesis by following a tempo of increasingly strong emphasis. In terms of action, the personification leads to stasis; in terms of the strength of feeling, the movement of the verse gathers steady impetus. Rhythm and rhetoric cooperate with Sidney's use of imagery for these effects. Finally, however formal the speaker's address may be as incipient action, it still fashions a context in which his emotions are part of an outward, moving, natural world. The third use to which personification may be put is basically satisfied.

The abundant, forceful, and extended treatment of feeling in these examples is more typical than not of Sidney's *Arcadia* verse, and it survives occasionally in *Astrophel and Stella*. But the cultivation of ornament is most general in the novel, no matter what the specific character of individual poems, laments, pleas, types of praise, incantation, angry or ecstatic outbursts. The modes of decorative style examined in this and the previous chapter have another common ground: behind them is the impulse to fuse all the deliberate elements of style for single effects. We seldom find Sidney's rhythm going in one direction, his rhetoric in another, and the structure of his imagery in still a third. They stand together, usually in one and the same place, unlike the elements in the poetry of Donne, whose meter joins a spontaneously colloquial rhythm to the highly patterned and complicated structure of his rhetoric or his imagery, or those in Shakespeare, whose occasionally very formal rhythms may coincide with the most daring and unexpected shifts in the ground of the imagery.[11]

As against these, Sidney's *Arcadia* verse exhibits a technique dedicated to sameness and completeness of effect. For this reason, many of his poems seem to lack complexity or tension. Unequipped to render a particular experience in depth, they tend to force love, or anger, or jealousy, or grief, into the most restricted and shaped patterns. From time to time Sidney does manage a variety of perspectives on a subject by the careful use of the logical places of comparison, contrast, or cause and effect, but in general the surface effect of his more ornate verse is uniform and uncomplicated, even where it displays the abundance of repetition. Fortunately, these limitations are not absolute.

[11] The phenomenon is familiar in most of Donne's lyrics; Shakespeare's Sonnet 129, "The expense of spirit in a waste of shame," carries the procedure to a successful extreme.

43

Paradoxically, one of Sidney's consciously and heavily patterned poems, the double sestina "You Gote-heard Gods," reaches surprising depths.

"You Gote-heard Gods" (*Works*, I, 141–143) is in the form of a dialogue between two young shepherds, Strephon and Klaius. The use of twelve stanzas and an envoy instead of the six normal to the sestina only intensifies the exotic and ingenious nature of that type of verse. The stanzas are inevitably repetitious of one another, using the same line endings, but in different orders. All the line endings are feminine, so that the falling rhythm is unvarying, a technique that Sidney exploits for rhythmic monotony in the translations of the *Psalms* and in several other poems in the *Arcadia*. If there is no rime, there is its analogy. There is, too, considerable grammatical matching of pairs of stanzas; the speakers vie in talking about the same things in the same way, and this effect is increased by the frequency of anaphora. The unflagging insistence of the rhythm is almost over-powering, for, as Empson justly remarks, "the poem beats, however rich its orchestration, with a wailing and immovable monotony, for ever upon the same doors in vain."[12] At the first reading the poem may seem, because of its monotony, only an exercise in sustainment of mood. Actually the effect is cumulative; consistent tempo assists a gradual increase in the vehemence of the speakers' feelings, moving from a simple statement of woefulness in the first two stanzas through "huge despaire" and heartbreak (stanzas 3 and 4), longing for death (stanzas 5–8), to potential madness (stanzas 9 and 10). What we have here is a simple progression of emotional distress whose stages are carefully blocked in by the stanzaic pattern. But this pattern serves only to announce one more inclusive, for the mounting emotional strain is an intensive prelude to announcement of its cause, amorous frustration:

Strephon For she, whose parts maintainde a perfect musique,
            Whose beautie shin'de more then the blushing morning,
            Who much did passe in state the stately mountaines,
            In straightnes past the Cedars of the forrests,
            Hath cast me wretch into eternall evening,
            By taking her two Sunnes from these darke vallies.

[12] *Seven Types of Ambiguity*, rev. ed. (New York, 1955), p. 44.

44

Klaius   For she, to whom compar'd, the Alpes are vallies,
        She, whose lest word brings from the spheares their musique,
        At whose approach the Sunne rose in the evening,
        Who, where she went, bare in her forhead morning,
        Is gone, is gone from these our spoyled forrests,
        Turning to desarts our best pastur'de mountaines.

                         (Stanzas 11–12)

The procedure emerges as broadly, but precisely, periodic, all stanzas but the envoy being in reality one long, stretched sentence. The envoy is an appended summary comment.

No more extreme or more classic instance of ornate amplification could be found. Suspension of the point to be made allows the richest intensity of mood to be worked in and carefully shaped as well. Moreover, analyzed thus far, the poem presents itself as an achievement in cooperating structures: stanza, linear rhythm, the matching of descriptive adjectives, the parallel stages of emotion endured by the speakers perfectly assist delay of statement, and all this Sidney accomplishes within the severe restrictions of the sestina, only doubling his problems by carrying it to twice its normal length. This poem seems to arrive at all the goals of Sidney's cultivation of symmetry and emphatic amplification, and it does so, I believe, more completely and effortlessly than any of the other *Arcadia* poems constructed on similar principles.

Yet it also reaches beyond these goals and manages a depth and complexity we should not expect. These further complications—both of mood and of meaning—are to be found, as Empson has discovered,[13] in Sidney's manipulation of the imagery. Not only are multiple and ambiguous associations attached to them, but they are also the vehicles for fluctuating, shifting perceptions of the relationships between the speakers or actors and their pastoral surroundings. Thus the role of the imagery changes from simple descriptiveness to pathetic fallacy to straight metaphor or conceit, and the result, whether Sidney meant it or not, is much more than a stress on emotions simply described as melancholy, despair, or frustration. To illustrate, the first stanza attaches more or less conventional epithets to the mountains, valleys, forest, morning, and evening, contrasting them with the speaker's "playning" music (the only image not drawn from nature). The epithets are, strictly speaking, pathetic fallacies, but such commonplace

---

[13] The same, pp. 44–45.

ones that they are scarcely noticeable. Not until "wofull vallies" in the second stanza (we already know that the speakers are "wofull") is the strategy emphatic. The opening of the third stanza is simple description of the normal mode of pastoral life, but there is a very quick switch in mid-stanza from scene painting or descriptive narration to metaphor:

> I that was once esteem'd for pleasant musique,
> Am banisht now among the monstrous mountaines
> Of huge despaire.
>
> (Stanza 3)

We anticipate real mountains and instead get figurative ones. At the same time, the inner condition of the speakers and their natural surroundings have merged and become confused (the same movement from description to trope occurs in stanza 4). In stanza 5 the identification persists, but then Klaius returns, momentarily, to a more realistic perception of the distinctness of himself and nature ("Long since I hate the night, more hate the morning"), only to lose himself once again in metaphor at the end of stanza 6. Even more radical is Strephon's statement in stanza 7:

> Me seemes I see the high and stately mountaines,
> Transforme themselves to lowe dejected vallies.

Nightingales begin to sing like owls, and the accustomed decorum of nature is overturned as Klaius follows suit. In stanzas 9 and 10, which in the order of emotional description are the most intense, Strephon and Klaius speak as if they had returned to a sane awareness of the disparateness of man and nature, and for the rest of the poem their metaphorical energies are spent objectively describing the perfection of the absent lady in the piece. The envoy personifies the mountains, forests, and valleys, but rather coolly so.

What has happened in this process is a much more profound and unorthodox revelation of the protagonists' psychology than is possible through the other structural elements. The rendering of near hysteria, or at least of the ways in which it affects perception of the world outside, is a genuine surprise, especially if one is familiar with Sidney's other patterned and effusive poems whose richness is available only on the surface. It could be argued, I suppose, that the need to use the same images over and over again in the same position in each line forced Sidney to vary their function, and that consequently whatever psychological acuity they release is accidental. I think, however, that the insights are more carefully planned; at least Sidney's language so indicates when he has both speakers say, "Me seemes," as they announce their own distorted visions. At any rate, I only wish to add that stylistically the poem still remains symmetrical, amplified, ornate, which should warn us that these qualities do not always force simplicity or intensity of statement alone. These results are merely the normal limits of amplified discourse as Sidney practices it in the *Arcadia* poems, and "You Gote-heard Gods" is a fine demonstration that limits exist to be transgressed.

4.

Ornate Style and the Cult of Idealistic Love

*T*he ingenious and decorative fulness of style examined so far is ubiquitous in some poets. Spenser almost never seems restrained in rhythm or figure, whether he is writing sonnet, epic, pastoral, or satire, whether his subject is love, despair, marriage, or courtly life. But the verse most generally typical of the Renaissance deals with love or with emotions akin to it, and the most prominent guise of love was Petrarchan. Sidney's *Arcadia*-poems contain some didactic pieces, two or three on marriage, some hymns, and some lightly satiric pieces, but generally he follows the disposition of his contemporaries and predecessors in giving his largest attention to the utterances of lovers and their mistresses. Love is the central symbol of the *Arcadia*, and its moments of lyric expression or interludes of pastoral debate follow the lead of the narrative in concentrating emotion and psychology in the same direction. For Sidney, perhaps, the coincidence of love and poetry was nearly inevitable, for although he complains, in *The Defence of Poesie*, that religious expression has been under-exploited, his own discussion of lyric turns naturally to the love poem.

48

That same discussion also complains of the excesses of ornate style, and the union of ornateness and the broad tradition associated with Petrarch is neither accidental nor temporary. The intense expressiveness of the poets of the *dolce stil nuovo*, usually an attempt to fuse metaphysical idealism and amorous passion, was modified and popularized by Petrarch and codified by his Italian and French followers into a tradition so strong that few poets could write amorous verse without reference to it. As late as the seventeenth century Donne and Herbert in their different ways felt the necessity of an explicit reaction against the Petrarchan manner. Petrarchism had entered the bloodstream of Italian and French literary convention, and in *Tottel's Miscellany* it joined hands with ornateness in English style. The history of Petrarchism is a long one, and its main features—its reliance on and alliance with courtly love and Platonic philosophy, its use as a vehicle for studied and stylized expression, and its perpetuation of formulas of attitude—are so familiar that they need only brief recapitulation here.[1] On the other hand, the extent and meaning of this tradition as they affect Sidney's verse are not wholly understood.

Sidney's use of the style and attitudes of Petrarchism was anything but indolent, automatic gesture. He was familiar with the more obvious motifs and clichés, and he used them.[2] But it is more noteworthy that Petrarchan psychology thoroughly permeates the prose narrative of the *Arcadia*, even in revision and even in a context where the only laudable goal of love is marriage. Proper and improper lovers alike worship their mistresses as ideal and unattainable. Only the matching of the pairs of lovers at the end violates the usually adulterous code of the Petrarchan situation. With this in mind we may easily take for granted those poems most obviously imitative of the tradition, and the close identification of Petrarchism and *Astrophel and Stella* may easily obscure its recognition in his other lyrics. Sidney is not necessarily at

[1] Lisle C. John's *The Elizabethan Sonnet Sequences* conveniently summarizes the main conventions of expression. Jefferson B. Fletcher's *The Religion of Beauty in Women*, 2nd ed., C. S. Lewis's *The Allegory of Love*, Alexander Denomy's *The Heresy of Courtly Love* (New York, 1947), and Louis B. Salomon's *The Rebellious Lover in English Poetry* (Philadelphia, 1931) should be consulted for the history and background of Renaissance amatory verse. Of a complex and difficult topic I emphasize only those portions central to Sidney's verse.

[2] *The Elizabethan Sonnet Sequences*, "Table of Conceits," pp. 195–200. See also Janet G. [Espiner-] Scott, *Les sonnets élisabéthains*, pp. 16 ff.

49

his best only when he departs from convention, nor is his sonnet sequence the only gauge of his poetic stature.

Petrarchan feeling centers in the conception of love as a type of religious worship, and at this point it joins Platonic philosophy. The *Phaedrus* and *Symposium* figure the lover's feelings as a kind of worship and suppose a dialectic of love as a cosmic force drawing the amorist to contemplate universal ideas of goodness and beauty: mortal love is the initial stage on the soul's journey back to its heavenly origins.[3] Historically Ficino's *Convito*, a commentary on the *Symposium*, initiates the explicit authority of Plato in Renaissance theories of love. Castiglione's equally influential *Courtier* is really a late arrival on the scene, but it epitomizes the Renaissance tendency to favor intellectualized and worshipful affection as necessary to social and religious refinement.[4] However, Dante had anticipated this development, allegorizing earthly passion and the adoration of womanly beauty as symbols of ecstatic religious contemplation,[5] and the long chronicle of Petrarch's *canzone* records the gradual transformation of his earthly (though unconsummated) passion for Laura into religious understanding.[6] At the same time, putting love to the service of philosophy and religion was not the only concern of the poets. Cavalcanti remained earthbound,[7] and later poets could borrow the language of the metaphysicians without any serious philosophical or religious motive. Du Bellay, in spite of his anti-Petrarchan outburst, is thoroughly pervaded by Platonistic concepts, especially in his *XIII Sonnetz de l'honnete amour*, but Ronsard remains more the courtly and polished lover. Interest in philosophy and metaphysics has faded until love is contemplated as merely analogous to worship. Symbol and allegory

[3] *Phaedrus*, 246, 250–252; *Symposium*, 206–207.

[4] *The Book of the Courtier* (1528), trans. Sir Thomas Hoby (1561), reprinted in *Three Renaissance Classics*, ed. Burton A. Milligan (New York, 1953), pp. 507–615, esp.

[5] Cf. *La vita nuova*, Sonnet 25 ("Oltre la spera, che più larga gira").

[6] A recurrent motif in *In vita di madonna Laura* is the conflict between the poet's religious hopes and his earthly love for Laura; see, for example, "Padre del ciel; dope i perduti giorni." *In morte* treats the gradual resolution of this conflict as passion evolves into religious feeling. As Miss John (pp. 172–173) notes, none of the English sonneteers follows Petrarch so far.

[7] His love poetry is both courtly and sensual. The following sonnets are typical: "Se mercè fosse amica a' mici desiri," "Certo mie rime a te mandar vogliendo," "Un amoroso sguardo spiritale," and "O tuche porti negli occhi sovento."

50

have modulated into hyperbole: Ronsard's ladies are "déeses," "angéligues," "étoiles," but his theme remains human love.[8] Desportes, one of the more thoroughgoing traditionalists of the Pléiade, is a late survival of the philosophical strain, addressing Diane and Hyppolite with the complaining humility of the standard Petrarchan lover but reading them as symbols of divine virtue and beauty, ideally remote and inhumanly chaste.[9]

On the whole, the English poets are far less interested in referring their emotions to the Platonic system, less inclined, except Spenser, to use religious terminology to manifest doctrine. The early translators of Petrarch, Howell, Sowthern, and Watson, as well as Sidney's followers Daniel and Drayton, seem content with the overstatements of the vocabulary of worship. As Miss John remarks, "Most of Petrarch's followers . . . use the images of *saint* and *angel* only in the manner of Petrarch's early sonnets as indicating merely superlative grace and beauty."[10] Against this background Sidney's practice is not quite so empty of meaning, nor for that matter should we reduce Daniel and Drayton to the level of Watson, for they are at least artists. But Sidney's appreciation of beauty is not called into being for the sake of philosophy. He is perfectly aware of the doctrinal sources of his language, but his works have other purposes than the symbolic coherence of du Bellay, Desportes, or Spenser.[11]

Yet, if Sidney is less the metaphysician than some Petrarchans, his treatment of love is nevertheless more informed than that of many by the rationalism to which the Platonic lover refers his feelings.[12] In the *Phaedrus* virtuous love demands the tempering of passion by reason,

[8] Du Bellay is attracted by the most intense Platonic emotion but repelled by the artificialities in Petrarchan literary convention. See *XIII Sonnetz de l'honneste amour* and "A une dame" ("Contre les Pétrarquistes"). Cf. Robert J. Clements, *Critical Theory and Practice of the Pléiade* (Cambridge, Massachusetts, 1942), pp. 23–31. Ronsard's enormous production of love poems defies easy summary. He reflects all the moods of the conventional lover, addressing his poems to several women, but the opening sonnet of *Le premier livre des amours,* "Qui voudra voir comme Amour me surmonte," is a fairly accurate introduction to his purposes.

[9] Desportes is thoroughly committed to a Platonic understanding of love; cf. Robert M. Burgess, *Platonism in Desportes* (Chapel Hill, 1954).

[10] *The Elizabethan Sonnet Sequences*, pp. 137–138.

[11] See *Amoretti*, Sonnets 8, 88.

[12] Sidney's familiarity with Plato is evident in *Astrophel and Stella*, Sonnets 5, 21, and 25, the latter being a clear rendering of Plato's notion of the affective powers of virtue (*Phaedrus*, 254–255).

which eventually conducts the soul towards heaven. The lover's reason prompts him to shrink from brutish sensuality, although he must still be propelled by desire. This rationalization was a commonplace in Renaissance treatises on love,[13] but verse in the Petrarchan mold shows less interest in the triumphs of reason than in the exhaustive, highly emotional expression of passion, adoration, and suffering, and the Petrarchans, although they conceive passion as an unreasoning power, take its measure as an ennobling, refining impulse unfortunately contradictory in its impact on the feelings. Petrarch himself only occasionally mentions the role of judgment in moments of joy or melancholy.[14] Sidney, on the other hand, is among the few considerable poets in the tradition to examine closely and articulately the interplay of reason and desire. In the prose text of the *Arcadia* Musidorus' and Pyrocles' amorous feelings are tested by the rational principle, and a number of the poems dwell on the same issue.[15]

But, for a study of the *Arcadia* poems, this feature of Sidney's debt to intellectual convention is less crucial than the suffering of the Petrarchan lover. His anguish is impressive, persistent, and acute, and these qualities—or more properly their intensity—mark one point of difference between the Petrarchan and Platonic, the poetic and philosophic, conceptions of love. Both Plato and Castiglione, to take the philosophic tradition at its beginning and maturity, contemplate a fairly swift reciprocation of the lover's feelings, and Plato even tolerates physical consummation.[16] Both, however, are chiefly interested in a state of emotion that has passed beyond the call of sexual desire. In contrast, the orthodox Petrarchan lover involves himself in an

[13] *The Book of the Courtier, Three Renaissance Classics*, pp. 603–605.

[14] Some poems note that passion impairs the judgment: cf. "Solo e pensoso i più deserti campi" and "Io son già stanco di pensar sí come." However, the impression made by Petrarch's treatment of the effects of love is best described as a general emotional and spiritual malaise.

[15] For example, see *Works*, I, 54–59 and these poems: "Transformd in shew, but more transformd in minde" (I, 76), "Come *Dorus*, come, let songs thy sorowes signifie" (I, 127–132), "In vaine, mine Eyes, you labour to amende" (I, 147), "Thou Rebell vile, come, to thy master yelde" (I, 339), "Dorus, tell me, where is thy wonted motion" (I, 340–344), and "Reason, tell me thy mind, if here be reason" (II, 236).

[16] *Phaedrus*, 256: "And probably not long afterwards his desire is accomplished." *Symposium*, 208–209, deplores sexual desire only if it is the exclusive end of love. Castiglione (*Three Renaissance Classics*, p. 603) rather patronizingly tolerates it as the inevitable weakness of young men.

adulterous, "courtly" relationship. His reward is at best a chaste kiss emblematic of grudging and condescending regard, although in weaker moments he may hope for complete union. Frustration, occasioned by the lady's chastity and disdain, accompanies him everywhere; indeed, it is absolutely necessary to the mystique of this form of experience. Religiously humble in the face of his lady's supreme virtue and transcendent beauty, the lover therefore finds much of her value in her elusiveness. She must remain physically and emotionally withdrawn to be ideally worthwhile. Furthermore, the lover needs an occasion for lament but one that does not violate his moral sensitivity. The Platonic lover, in so far as he is distinct from the Petrarchan, finds his conflict less in frustration than in his attempt to apply the reins of reason to passion, and part of Sidney's uniqueness is that he manages to wed these two motifs rather naturally into his portraits of the effects of love. The shepherds Strephon and Klaius ask of Urania, "Hath not shee throwne reason upon oure desires, and, as it were given eyes unto *Cupid*?" (*Works*, I, 8). But loveliness may inflict pain, as Musidorus testifies in relating his first vision of Pamela: "For here (and no where els) did his infected eyes make his minde know, what power heavenly beauty hath to throw it downe to hellish agonies" (the same, I, 161).

But if Sidney can stress the rational element in the worship of beauty, he can more feelingly render its religious impulse, which in company with the motif of frustration gave rise to the formulas of descriptive imagery in the work of the Italian poets. The Petrarchan lover commonly protested the strength of his affection by praising his lady's features in the most beatific language. Her eyes were stars or suns, her hair golden wire, her skin ivory; her voice was the music of the spheres, and all her actions were those of a goddess. Conversely, the lover roasted in the fires of hell or was frozen by his lady's chaste disdain; his torments were the wounds of battle or siege warfare (both his lady and Cupid might be his enemies), while the ambivalent mixture of pain and joy in his heart might be described as a civil war; his passions so exhausted him that he was frequently on the verge of death; and yet night, its absence of light symbolic of death, was only an occasion for vivid images of his lady to inhabit his mind.[17] The most casual reading of the Italian, French, or English Petrarchans

[17] *The Elizabethan Sonnet Sequences*, "Table of Conceits," pp. 195–200.

makes plain their constant use of these formulas. And because the habit of these poets is to conceive love as continuous emotional extravagance, their verse is largely innocent of restraint of feeling or expression.

Long-standing and firmly conventional forms of expression are one motive for the ornate style of the *Arcadia* poems. But there are more precise causes to be found in Sidney's own presentation of idealized love. I have said that he does not allegorize love as transcendental religious yearning in the manner of Dante or record its evolution towards piety in the manner of Petrarch, but for Sidney love is, nevertheless, a mode of worship. The difference is that for him beauty and virtue never become totally and exclusively symbolic. They prompt impulses identical or similar to those associated with religious adoration, which in its turn informs the language of amorous praise. The little poem that follows holds a clear distinction between heaven and earth, but heavenly conceit translates the speaker's emotion:

> Why doost thou haste away
> O *Titan* faire the giver of the daie?
> Is it to carry newes
> To Westerne wightes, what starres in East appeare?
> Or doost thou thinke that heare
> Is left a Sunne, whose beames thy place may use?
> Yet stay and well peruse,
> What be her giftes, that make her equall thee,
> Bend all thy light to see
> In earthly clothes enclosde a heavenly sparke.
> Thy running course cannot such beawties marke:
> No, no, thy motions bee
> Hastened from us with barre of shadow darke,
> Because that thou the author of our sight
> Distainst we see thee staind with others light.
> (*Works*, II, 32)

The conceit is typical of the tradition of praise. The religious affinity of the lover's adoration lends it dignity. Here Sidney foregoes rhythmical and rhetorical ornateness, but his imagery betrays its origins in the convention of stately and stylized feeling. Moreover, Sidney's careful distinction between the lady and the scheme of things that provides the imagery by which she is valued reminds us that we are to recognize and perhaps approve an attitude towards her *like* our reverence for the "author of our sight." Worship and praise are analogous, but not identified.

"*Phaebus* farewell, a sweeter Saint I serve," uses a similar conceit and is also convenient for setting off Sidney's verse from the sort that manages only an empty parade of standard formulas of epithet and hyperbole. Apollo is the deity of the Arcadians, and Basilius, the speaker in the poem, introduces him with this account of his feelings: "O Goddesse [Zelmane], said hee towardes whom I have the greatest feeling of Religion, be not displeased at some shew of devotion I have made to *Apollo*: since he (if he know any thing) knowes that my harte beares farre more awful reverĕce to your self then to his, or any other the like *Deity*." The poem echoes this attitude:

> She heav'n on earth with beauties doth preserve.
> Thy beames I like, but her cleare rayes I love:
> Thy force I feare, her force I still do prove.
> (*Works*, II, 5)

Basilius' worship is, to be sure, so excessive as to amount to a perversion of both love and religion—to Zelmane it is like "the operation of a poyson" (the same, II, 6). In *Astrophel and Stella* a similar transference of devotion from heaven to earth, quite a different matter from worshiping the deity *through* the medium of earthly beauty and virtue, leads Astrophel to question the moral validity of his feelings. However, meditation is not the business of the *Arcadia* poems, for they turn, like the excerpt above, on ritualistic feeling and expression.

The error of Basilius as error is underlined not in the poem but in the surrounding context. Otherwise the psychology of his attitude is an extension of that common to all modes of love in the *Arcadia* and in the sequence. The shepherd Dorus (one of the heroes, Musidorus, in disguise) praises his lady in every other stanza of the pastoral, "Come *Dorus*, come, let songs thy sorowes signifie," and its quality is that of passionate and adoring celebration:

> O happie Gods, which by inward assumption
> Enjoy her soule, in bodies faire possession,
> And keepe it joynde, fearing your seates consumption.
>   How oft with raine of teares skies make confession,
> Their dwellers rapt with sight of her perfection

55

> From heav'nly throne to her heav'n use digression?
>   Of best things then what world can yeeld confection
> To liken her? Decke yours with your comparison:
> She is her selfe, of best things the collection.[18]
>
> (*Works*, I, 128)

Elsewhere he alludes to her perfection in these terms: "What circle then in so rare force beares swaye?" (the same, I, 130). Dorus's expression is just as conceited as that of Basilius and, strictly speaking, just as sacrilegious, and yet it is not, in the context of the novel, immoral or perverse. To endow love with the language and attitudes of religious worship does not seem to be the real measure of blame or approval; rather the adoration of an image of perfection who is at the same time a human being emerges as a prime ingredient in love of all kinds and appears in a great variety of poems, whether the lover is Musidorus intoning,

> You that are borne to be the worldes eye,
>
> (*Works*, II, 26)

or Astrophel, extolling Stella:

> Who hath the eyes which marrie state with pleasure,
> Who keepes the key of Natures chiefest treasure:
> To you, to you, all song of praise is due,
> Only for you the heav'n forgate all measure.
>
> (*First Song*)

The lover's abject humility is allied to his worship of perfection and is humanly consistent with it. Dorus finds, even though common sense tells him to look for more mundane objects to love, "Her eyes so maistering me, that such objection / Seemde but to spoyle the foode of thoughts long famished" (*Works*, I, 129), and in the same poem he dwells on his own empty, worthless mortality. The contrast is central and persistent in the Petrarchan verse of the *Arcadia* and *Astrophel and Stella* (in the latter it is relieved by irony and a searching explora-

---

[18] A casual and empty use of the religious motif is illustrated by William Percy, *Sonnets to the Faire Coelia* (1594), Sonnet 15: "What is her face so angel-like? *Angel-like.* / Then unto saints in mind sh'is not unlike. *Unlike.*" Like Sidney, Ronsard liberally employs religious conceits to clarify the lover's state of mind, as well as to intensify praise, but his reference is more persistently classical than Sidney's; see *Le premier livre des amours*, Sonnet 13, *et passim*.

tion of the values of idealistic devotion). One of the songs in the
Certaine Sonets, "O Faire, ô sweet, when I do looke on thee," neatly
combines the lover's sense of his lady's exaltedness with his own in-
feriority, forming something of a paradox of their union:

> O Faire, ô sweet, when I do looke on thee,
> In whom all joyes so well agree,
> Heart and soule do sing in me.
>> This you heare is not my tongue,
>> Which once said what I conceaved,
>> For it was of use bereaved,
>> With a cruell answer stong.
>>> No, though tongue to roofe be cleaved,
>>> Fearing least he chastisde be,
>>> Heart and soule do sing in me.

Besides fear, contemplation of supreme beauty and worth may inspire
"service"; Musidorus addresses a tree by carving a poem in its bark:

> Yet yeeld your graunt, a baser hand may leave
> His thoughtes in you, where so sweete thoughtes were spent,
> For how would you the mistresse thoughts bereave
> Of waiting thoughts all to her service ment?

> (*Works*, II, 25)

More fully spelled out, the impulse to adore and serve high worth
yields a positive fruit in correct behavior.[19] So Astrophel justifies
himself in Sonnet 14:

> If that be sinne which doth the maners frame,
>> Wel staid with truth in word and faith of deed,
>> Readie of wit and fearing nought but shame:
> If that be sinne which in fixt hearts doth breed
>> A loathing of all loose unchastitie,
>> Then Love is sinne, and let me sinfull be.

So, too, Dorus admits that "errour lies oft in zeale," but maintains
that he is "of true hart" (*Works*, I, 343).

These impulses all lead to hyperbole, often to a hymn-like redundancy and overstatement, but it would be mistaken to regard the style
thus occasioned as necessarily an excess of language alone. Rather it is

---

[19] The concept of service is, of course, chivalric and therefore older than
Petrarchism.

a language that belongs with certain modes of feeling. These are not merely intense; they are intensely worshipful. And in such a context too much familiarity of expression would alter, or even frustrate, the sense that the lady one adores is a divine work of art. As a formal (if still human) object she must be contemplated and celebrated formally.

Otherwise described, Sidney's presentation of idealistic and idealized love is more than connoisseurship; it is a total commitment. The psychological reverberations felt by the two speakers, Strephon and Klaius, in "You Gote-heard Gods" affect their entire existence and their entire world. Because "she is gone," they cannot see joy or light or order within themselves or in their surroundings. And according to Dorus,

> Thus she is framde: her eyes are my direction;
> Her love my life; her anger my destruction.
> Lastly what so she is, that's my protection.
>
> (*Works*, I, 342)

Astrophel, from time to time, feels himself utterly engulfed by his attraction for Stella. He sees all his "good" in her (Sonnet 60), and in Sonnet 48 brings together a full statement of the terms of his allegiance:

> Soules joy, bend not those morning starres from me,
>   Where Vertue is made strong by Beauties might,
>   Where *Love* is chastnesse, Paine doth learne delight,
>   And Humblenesse growes one with Majestie.
>
> What ever may ensue, ô let me be
>   Copartner of the riches of that sight:
>   Let not mine eyes be hel-driv'n from that light:
>   O looke, ô shine, ô let me die and see.

The religious commitment of Sidney's lovers, with their sense of unworthiness, their hunger for a consuming perfection, and their need to feel intensely and totally, is a distinct attitude. I should say at once that *Astrophel and Stella* differs from the *Arcadia* poems in offering a critique of this idealism, but its expression is still to be found there. In the *Arcadia* poems, particularly those attributed to Pyrocles (Zelmane) and Musidorus (Dorus), the heroes of the novel, the strain is more constant. And whatever the circumstances of the narrative, the

58

poems bear the impression that they are fashioned to bestow incessant praise on someone human but unapproachable. The parade of heavenly images is, to be sure, convention, but, judged by its effects, it makes abstractions of the ladies described, or at least isolates them as expressions of a particular state of mind. Love in certain, but not all, guises is a worship of the impossible and demands expression in measured incantation. Pyrocles loves a flesh and blood Philoclea, but his poetic eulogy offers symmetrically formal expression to a vision of symmetry:

> Thus hath each part his beauties part,
> But how the Graces doo impart
> To all her limmes a spetiall grace,
> Becomming every time and place.
> Which doth even beautie beautifie,
> And most bewitch the wretched eye.
> How all this is but a faire Inne
> Of fairer guestes, which dwell within.
> Of whose high praise, and praisefull blisse,
> Goodnes the penne, heaven paper is.
> The inke immortall fame doth lende:
> As I began, so must I ende.
> No tongue can her perfections tell,
> In whose each part all tongues may dwell.
>
> (*Works*, I, 222)

These lines, the conclusion to a long and ample blazon, recall the usual alliance between idealizing love—one that grasps its object as harmoniously proportioned—and a balanced and ample style. Where the praising verse of the *Arcadia* is most Petrarchan, most within an extremely formal tradition, its style sets emotional and psychological reality most at a distance. Unlike Donne's persuasive lyrics, even more cosmic in the range of their imagery but at the same time more firmly rooted in a circumstantial reality from which idea and emotion grow, Sidney's poems find their setting outside themselves in the prose narrative of the novel. As I have suggested, they are performances of a special kind of stylized feeling, and there is evidence that Sidney was alive to other possibilities. Thus, for contrast, there is a poem in *Certaine Sonets* listed as a translation from Montemayor's *Diana*. The stanza I quote is conceited, and thus sufficiently indirect, but the praise is restrained, partially simplified by the conceit, and the setting and manner of the verse are almost casual:

> The same *Sireno* in Montemajor holding his mistresse
>   glasse before her, looking upon her while she
>   viewed her selfe, thus sang:

> Of this high grace with blisse conjoyn'd
>   No further debt on me is laid,
>   Since that in selfe same mettall coin'd,
>   Sweet Ladie you remaine well paid.
>   For if my place give me great pleasure,
>   Having before me Natures treasure,
>   In face and eyes unmatched being,
>   You have the same in my hands seeing,
>   What in your face mine eyes do measure.

The language of wit and understatement subdues emotional extravagance to the working out of the idea, however trivial, and feeling becomes an after effect, not a surface effusion.

In the *Arcadia*, nevertheless, the praise of women is largely worship of ideal, or at least idealized, beings, and its intensity is usually ceremonial. Equally conventional and equally formal is the lover's suffering, which is, if anything, more pervasive than adoring praise. Furthermore, suffering grows directly out of humility and the overpowering sense of the lady's worth and inaccessibility, although some poems lament the inward effects of love without reference to its object. On the other hand, pain influenced by frustrated desire and a strong sense of unworthiness, although it may rail against the chaos of disturbed emotions, will blame and adore its cause in the same breath. Strephon and Klaius, both in love with the absent Urania, lament their condition at some length in "I Joye in griefe, and doo detest all joyes." Following descriptions of melancholy and its effects come three summary stanzas:

> *Klaius* Thus, thus, I had, alas, my losse in chase,
>   When first that crowned *Basiliske* I knewe,
>   Whose footesteps I with kisses oft did trace,
>   Till by such hap, as I must ever rewe,
>   Mine eyes did light upon her shining hewe,
>   And hers on me, astonisht with that sight.
>   Since then my harte did loose his wonted place,

> Infected so with her sweet poysons might,
> That, leaving me for dead, to her it went:
> But ah her flight hath my dead reliques spent.

Strephon But ah her flight hath my dead reliques spent,
> Her flight from me, from me, though dead to me
> Yet living still in her, while her beames lent
> Such vitall sparke, that her mine eyes might see.
> But now those living lights absented be,
> Full dead before, I now to dust should fall,
> But that eternall paines my soule should hent,
> And keepe it still within this body thrall:
> That thus I must, while in this death I dwell,
> In earthly fetters feele a lasting hell.

Klaius In earthly fetters feele a lasting hell
> Alas I doo; from which to finde release,
> I would the earth, I would the heavens fell.
> But vaine it is to thinke these paines should cease,
> Where life is death, and death cannot breed peace.
> O faire, ô onely faire, from thee, alas,
> These foule, most foule, distresses to me fell;
> Since thou from me (ô me) ô Sunne didst passe.
> Therefore esteeming all good blessings toyes
> I joy in griefe, and doo detest all joyes.
>
>   (*Works*, I, 351)

The paradox that the liveliness of love is a form of death, or, in other terms, that the lady's vitality causes a symbolic death, adopts the language of religious estrangement, recalling perhaps the Christian view of man's dual nature, the mortality of his flesh and the immortality of his soul. Present, also, is a specific cause for this condition: Klaius declares that he has been bereft of his heart which is "Infected so with her sweet poysons might." It is worth adding that the extravagance of expression, its emphatic redundancy ("O faire, ô onely faire"), and the hyperbole of its descriptive images, match that of "You Gote-heard Gods," another and more perfectly fashioned ejaculation of pain.[20]

This lament is standard and reports melancholy in terms of the "contraries."[21] It contains an essential motif of Petrarchan idealism: the necessary frustration of the lover who turns to a model of perfec-

[20] See the discussion at the end of Chapter 3.
[21] *The Elizabethan Sonnet Sequences*, p. 197.

tion. His pain and suffering must match in intensity the quality of his lady's beauty and virtue. Love is cast in the form of an equation defining the depth and limits of the experience, whether the specific descriptive terms are wounds, fire, disease, healing, killing, warfare, tears, sighs, light, or darkness. The lover, always hungry for divine excellence, must always content himself with frustrated despair, and these two conditions circumscribe his universe. In the prose narrative of the *Arcadia*, Pyrocles and Musidorus eventually find release in marriage, but this does not alter the vision of the laments assigned to them and to others. The poems are fragments, as it were, not a complete cycle, but among them they have an impressive consistency. In only a few is there any shift in the values of melancholy: their movement is more properly rhetorical, a development of a single theme in terms either of intensity—as "You Gote-heard Gods" whose successive stanzas add richness to and magnify the speakers' declamation of their loss—or in terms of rounding out a state of emotion already given, its presence and specific meaning taken for granted. I should except, of course, some pieces which might properly be called lover's laments and in which there are distinct changes in attitude or situation. Such is "Ring out your belles" from *Certaine Sonets*: its final stanza reverses the opening declaration that love is dead. Different also are the Fourth and Fifth Songs from *Astrophel and Stella*, which carry narrative and reversal of attitude some distance. The latter two, although they render Astrophel's frustration, go well beyond the usual Petrarchan complaint. But the fixity and lack of dramatic interest or progress of the laments in the *Arcadia* is their most distinguishing quality. They arrest the movement of the novel—as do most of its other poems—much as if a dramatically vivid piece were frozen into a *tableau vivant*: against their setting and background they lead virtually an independent life.

The emotional stasis common to these laments is also an excuse, if not a justification, for the amplitude and symmetry of style found in them. If we accept the usual reasons given by the rhetoricians in favor of an ornate style—its superior persuasiveness, its ability to make emotionally acceptable what is already known—then it is not hard to see a motive in Sidney's use of devices of emphasis and overemphasis, the qualities to which his ornateness most often leads. Heavy ornament is further appropriate for the particular qualities of emotional presentation I have been describing in this chapter: violent melancholy and adoration of supreme virtue would seem naturally to demand overstatement and fullness in their expression, for these are, after all, strong passions. Only the contours of rhetoric and rhythm contain them, and yet these are apt to be just as emphatic as they are limiting and controlling. If the need of the listener or reader to recognize and delight in the shape of the period or balance of the stanza forces the poet to bring it to an end or to adopt a preconceived form, these devices also allow and encourage the marathon of hyperbole.

5.

The Theory of Artless Style

$\mathcal{S}$idney's critical statements about lyric point in two directions. On the one hand, they seem to betray an intention to dismantle the principles of style implicit in the *Arcadia* poems, the translations of the *Psalms*, and a few of the *Certaine Sonets*. The *Defence of Poesie* was probably composed after most, if not all, of the *Arcadia* verse was completed. As he lists his objections to over-decorative lyric, Sidney confesses himself "sicke among the rest." On the other hand, the *Defence* is echoed in a number of sonnets in *Astrophel and Stella* which argue against conventional devices in lyric ornament and urge a plainer, more direct style, and had the sequence carried out this program with utter and obvious fidelity to its new principles, the work of the critic would be simpler than it is. Perhaps, indeed, criticism would be unnecessary. But *Astrophel and Stella* does not abandon the devices familiar in the *Arcadia* poems, and while the sequence does speak with a different voice, it does not represent the sharp, absolute break with ornateness that some of its own poems would suggest.

Nevertheless, the differences between *Astrophel and Stella* and most of the remainder of Sidney's poetry are real and important, and the first place to read them is in Sidney's critical remarks on lyric style. Coming near the end of the *Defence of Poesie*, his discussion of the

"Lyricall kind of Songs and Sonets" rests upon a close analogy to prose oratory; indeed he makes the contact between the two realms of expression so intimate that he resorts to general stylistic principles again and again to argue against one tradition and promote another. What is proscriptive in his discussion develops into an attack on Ciceronian imitation; more positively, he places himself in the camp of the anti-Ciceronians and supports a style more directly prompted by naked truth, and more deliberately committed to a surface of casual, transparent expression.

The anti-Ciceronian reaction in the Renaissance began effectively with Erasmus' *Ciceronianus* (1528), an ironic conversation in which two of the speakers toy rather cruelly with the extreme biases of an unimaginative imitator of Cicero. In England John Jewel and Sir Thomas Elyot argued against the excesses of an elaborately formal, monotonously periodic style as hostile to clear meanings, and when the reforms of Peter Ramus reached England, they gave further authority to such suggestions, narrowing the traditional difference between logic and rhetoric.[1] Furthermore, Ramus encouraged a simplified view of the details of rhetorical theory and laid stress on those devices of style which might make it intellectually more rigorous and plain.[2] But Ciceronianism died hard, if it died at all in the sixteenth century. Equally powerful voices saw anti-Ciceronianism as the abandonment of all effective style, and Ascham, a writer who often sacrificed ornament to trenchancy, could nevertheless complain, "Ye know not what hurt ye do to learning, that care not for wordes but for matter, and so make a deuorse betwixt the tongue and the hart."[3] But even without the aid of Ramism the main tendency of English rhetorical thinking was beginning to lean towards plainness, towards a distrust of the ample means to decorative persuasion. Ralph Lever complained of "Ciceroni-

---

[1] In one sense, of course, Ramus helped divorce logic and rhetoric, for he bereft the latter of all but two of its topics, style and delivery; but at the same time writers following Ramistic theory were drawn to logic for an understanding of invention, disposition, and the like. See Wilbur S. Howell, *Logic and Rhetoric in England, 1500–1700* (Princeton, 1956), Chap. IV; Rosemund Tuve, *Elizabethan and Metaphysical Imagery* (Chicago, 1947), pp. 252, 281–282, 319–323, and Chap. XII.

[2] Rosemund Tuve, *loc. cit.*, and Perry Miller, *The New England Mind, The Seventeenth Century* (New York, 1939), Appendix A, "The Literature of Ramus' Logic in Europe."

[3] "Of Imitation," *Elizabethan Critical Essays*, I, 6.

ans & suger tongued fellowes, which labour more for finenes of speach, then for knowledge of good matter,"[4] and Thomas Wilson, in many respects traditionally Ciceronian, nevertheless claimed to prefer the "playne familier maner of wryting and speakyng" of Demosthenes to "the large veyne and vehement maner of eloquence" attributed to Cicero.[5] The truth was that many stylists felt that the Ciceronians had gone too far, that their interest in words and rhythms and images amounted to obsessive idolatry. The Ciceronian cult of full and measured eloquence was suspected of concealing ignorance and emptiness under a supposed beauty of language, and its opponents, epitomized by Elyot, sought to back their pleas for restraint by urging the necessity, even the pre-eminence, of solid thinking:

> But if he that speketh doo lacke that knowledge howe so euer the beautye of his wordes and rayson shall content the eares of them that be ignorant, yet therof shall come to them but litell profit.[6]

The favorable reception of Ramism at Cambridge and its effect on the thinking of Abraham Fraunce suggest conditions for Sidney's anti-Ciceronianism. In his *Lawiers Logike* (1588) Fraunce announces their common interest in Ramistic logic "almost seaven yeares now ouergone" and mentions the *Arcadia*, among other works, as showing "the true effectes of natural Logike" in contrast to the abuses of "those miserable *Sorbonists*."[7] The debt of his *Arcadian Rhetorike* (1588) to Sidney for quotation and to Ramus and Omer Talon for method is familiar.[8] Evidently Fraunce thought Sidney's prose and verse sufficiently perspicuous to be set against tradition in both logic and rhetoric. But to trace the specific effects of Ramism in Sidney's writings is another matter: Ramus offered a theoretical reform of logic and rhetoric, while Sidney's concern was for a perspicuous style and he echoed a number of non-Ramistic sources.[9] Ramism may only be tentatively

---

[4] *The Arte of Reason, rightly termed, Witcraft* (1573), sig. *5ʳ⁻ᵛ. Cited by Howell, *Logic and Rhetoric in England, 1500–1700*, p. 62.

[5] *The Three Orations of Demosthenes chiefe Orator among the Grecians, in fauour of the Olynthians* (1570), sig. *iiiiᵛ.

[6] *Of the Knowledge which Maketh a Wise Man* (1533), facsimile, ed. Edwin J. Howard (Oxford, Ohio, 1946), sig. Dᵛ, p. 17.

[7] *The Lawiers Logike exemplifying the praecepts of Logike by the practise of the common Lawe* (1588), sig. lʳ.

[8] Ed. Ethel Seaton (Oxford, 1950).

[9] Wilson, Harvey, or Erasmus are strong possibilities. Sidney had practiced translating Cicero; see his letter to Languet of 18 February 1574, *Works*, III, 83.

classified as one of the many forces urging Sidney to object to excessive ornamentation in verse.[10]

What is certain is that the tradition of anti-Ciceronianism, in its insistence upon the persuasive values of thought filtered through relatively informal style, surrounds Sidney's literary maturity. He was, for example, associated with Gabriel Harvey, and in 1577 Harvey brought out his *Ciceronianus*, a work reflecting both the anti-Ciceronianism of Erasmus, with its objections to rigid imitation, and the teachings of Ramus, with their steady emphasis on a thoughtful order of discourse and the consequent need for restraint of ornament. In the dedicatory epistle Harvey says that his work is "stripped of all rhetorical copiousness and glorying more in its furniture of subject matter than in its parade of words," and in the essay itself he laments his former Ciceronianism:

Why should I tell how great and simon-pure a Ciceronian I was at that time in the choice of every single word, in the composition and structure of sentences, in the discriminating use of cases and tenses, in the symmetry of cut-and-dried phrases, in the shaping of sentence-divisions and clauses, in the rhythmical measuring of periods, in the variety and smoothness of clausulae, in the careful and elaborate multiplication of all sorts of refinements. . . . I valued words more than content, language more than thought, the one art of speaking more than the thousand subjects of knowledge. . . . I believed that the bone and sinew of imitation lay in my ability to choose as many brilliant and elegant words as possible, to reduce them into order, and to connect them together in a rhythmical period.[11]

In preferring a style shorn of symmetry and uncluttered by the writer's hunt for elegance and embellishment, Harvey wishes to "unite

[10] Critics seeking a motive for the plain style and logical toughness of some Elizabethan and of Metaphysical verse in the reforms of Ramus are cautioned by Walter J. Ong, *Ramus, Method, and the Decay of Dialogue* (Cambridge, Massachusetts, 1958), p. 286: "The apparent collusion between Ramist dialectic and rhetoric and the habits of thought and imagination of Elizabethan poets testifies to common background rather than to any conscious sympathy." Father Ong also notes (p. 287) a serious difference between Ramistic method and that of the poets: "The overtones of 'real' or colloquial speech, that is, of *dialogue* between persons, which sixteenth- and seventeenth-century poetry specializes in, give it its characteristic excellence. Ramist rhetoric, on the other hand, is not a dialogue rhetoric at all, and Ramist dialectic has lost all sense of Socratic dialogue and even most sense of scholastic dispute."

[11] Trans. Clarence A. Forbes, *U. of Nebraska Studies in the Humanities*, no. 4 (November, 1945), pp. 63, 69.

dialectic and knowledge with rhetoric, thought with language."[12] In company with his predecessors and followers, he was in effect seeking to make current the principles described by Cicero for the classical plain style. Cicero views the plain orator as one who neglects the obvious resources of rhythm, affects a studied carelessness in method and organization, uses short and concise clauses in place of the period, favors maxims over other forms of ornament ("in metaphor will be modest, sparing in the use of archaisms"), and avoids clauses of similar length with like endings or identical cadences.[13] Cicero is especially careful to emphasize a casual, informal texture in the plain style, precisely the qualities sought by Montaigne and Bacon, two of the most influential of its practitioners. Among poets Jonson is the most clearly influenced by this point of view, which also informs the anti-Petrarchism and the emerging satire of the 1590's.[14]

Against this background, *The Defence of Poesie* shows itself consistent with most of the aims of the anti-Ciceronians. Sidney pays little attention to maxims, but he is specific about the restraint of noticeable ornament, the avoidance of neologisms and far-fetched metaphor, the omission of clauses of equal length and *similiter cadenses*, and other devices leading to what Cicero calls "elaborate symmetry and a certain grasping after a pleasant effect." In treating the faults and possibilities of lyric style in his own time Sidney rejects, in theory at least, all ornament used for its own sake and does so with an eye to the oratorical principles laid down by the anti-Ciceronians. As he remarks, poetry and oratory are alike in "the wordish consideration."

Behind the analogy to oratory is the assumption that all discourse, poetic and otherwise, must be persuasive, and Sidney opens his discussion of the "*Lyricall* kind of Songs and Sonets" on this note, complaining that most such verse is unconvincing and mechanical when involved in hyperbole:

But truly many of such writings, as come under the banner of unresistable love, if I were a mistresse, would never perswade mee they were in love: so

[12] The same, p. 83.

[13] *Orator* (Loeb Classical Library), Sects. 76–85.

[14] According to Wesley Trimpi, "The Classical Plain Style and Ben Jonson's Poems," (Harvard University diss., 1957), p. 4, "The Senecan influence and the anti-Petrarchan reaction of the satirical poets of the 1590's are the two main Renaissance movements in the development of the classical plain style in English poetry." I am in Mr. Trimpi's debt for many suggestions in this chapter.

coldly they applie firie speeches, as men that had rather redde lovers writings, and so caught up certaine swelling Phrases, which hang togither like a man that once tolde me the winde was at Northwest, and by South, because he would be sure to name winds inough, then that in truth they feele those passions, which easily as I thinke, may be bewraied by that same forciblenesse or *Energia*.[15]

Energia, the impressiveness of the idea shorn of embellishment, is therefore related to the problem of sincerity (or its appearance, which is what matters if one wants to be most persuasive) to the extent that wholesale ornamentation obscures both. Sidney wants a poet who, like Cicero's plain orator, would give more attention to thought than to words.

The body of his attack on overdecorative style lists affected eloquence, exotic imagery, and its too liberal use in similitude as particular vices:

So these men bringing in such a kinde of eloquence, well may they obtaine an opinion of a seeming finenesse, but perswade few, which should be the ende of their finenesse. Now for similitudes in certain Printed discourses, I thinke all Herberists, all stories of beasts, foules, and fishes, are rifled up, that they may come in multitudes to waite upon any of our conceits, which certainly is as absurd a surfet to the eares as is possible. For the force of a similitude not being to prove anything to a contrary disputer, but onely to explaine to a willing hearer, when that is done, the rest is a moste tedious pratling, rather overswaying the memorie from the purpose whereto they were applied, then anie whit enforming the judgement alreadie either satisfied, or by similitudes not to be satisfied.[16]

Sidney is anxious here, and throughout the *Defence*, to affirm the value of lyric as a medium for truth, and this motive lies behind his echoing of Cicero in the matter of restraining the volume of metaphor. As for love poets, to repeat, he hopes "that in truth they feele those passions."

Such a notion, perhaps somewhat wistfully voiced in an age of Petrarchan imitation (from which Sidney himself was not immune), informs those sonnets in *Astrophel and Stella* meditating poetic style.[17] It has been argued that these poems do not represent Sidney's own convictions because the style of the sequence so obviously employs devices Astrophel pretends to scorn and because protesting his sincerity

---

[15] *Works*, III, 41.   [16] The same, III, 42–43.
[17] Sonnets 1, 3, 6, 15, 28, 34, 44, 50, and 55.

is the conventional stance of the Petrarchan lover. According to this interpretation the critical sonnets are merely "stage" properties, included as part of the fiction in which the lover justifies his passion.[18] But such a theory is not needed to absolve Sidney from the charge of violating his own theories of composition. It is true that he never wholly emerges from the habit of echoing Petrarch and the formulas of the Petrarchan tradition, just as it is also true that he never discards rhetorical symmetry and ornamentation completely. But *Astrophel and Stella* is an effort in the direction of change, and it is especially significant because it employs the usual devices of style for purposes which do not appear or which are unripened in the *Arcadia* verse. The critical sonnets, especially because they accord so neatly with remarks in the *Defence*, have more than a casual bearing on that effort.

Collectively they are a protest that Astrophel means what he says and that he is expressing himself as directly and plainly as he can. So arguing, he carps at other poets on precisely the same grounds Sidney uses against the euphuists and Ciceronians in the *Defence*:

> You that do search for everie purling spring,
>> Which from the ribs of old *Parnassus* flowes,
>> And everie floure not sweet perhaps, which growes
>> Neare thereabouts, into your Poesie wring.
>
> You that do Dictionaries methode bring
>> Into your rimes, running in ratling rowes:
>> You that poore *Petrarchs* long deceased woes,
>> With new-borne sighes and denisend wit do sing.
>
> You take wrong waies those far-fet helpes be such,
>> As do bewray a want of inward tuch:
>> And sure at length stolne goods do come to light.
>> (Sonnet 15)

What Astrophel condemns is not tradition, but the unimaginative abuse of it. In like fashion he objects to an abundance of trite ornament ("everie purling spring," "everie floure"). Wholesale borrowings and the forcing of unnecessary rhythms and images upon the material blur the truth, and Astrophel's sneer at "daintie wits" implies a similar bias against a cultivated indirectness:

[18] Hallett Smith, *Elizabethan Poetry*, pp. 144–145, 151–152.

Let daintie wits crie on the Sisters nine,
  That bravely maskt, their fancies may be told:
  Or *Pindares* Apes,[19] flaunt they in phrases fine,
  Enam'ling with pied flowers their thoughts of gold:

Or else let them in statelier glorie shine,
  Ennobling new found Tropes with problemes old:
  Or with strange similies enrich each line,
  Of herbes or beastes, which *Inde* or *Afrike* hold.
                                    (Sonnet 3)

In similar terms the *Defence* notes the prostitution of contemporary
lyric style and specifically calls attention to the presence of the same
vices in prose discourse of the Ciceronian variety:

Now, for the outside of it, which is words, or (as I may tearme it) *Diction*,
it is even well worse: so is it that hony-flowing Matrone *Eloquence*, appar-
relled, or rather disguised, in a Courtisanlike painted affectation. One time
with so farre fet words, that many seeme monsters, but must seeme straungers
to anie poore Englishman: an other time with coursing of a letter, as if they
were bound to follow the method of a Dictionary: an other time with figures
and flowers, extreemlie winter-starved. . . . Truly I could wish, if at least I
might be so bold to wish, in a thing beyond the reach of my capacity, the dili-
gent Imitators of *Tully & Demosthenes*, most worthie to be imitated, did not
so much keepe *Nizolian* paper bookes of their figures and phrases, as by
attentive translation, as it were, devoure them whole, and make them wholly
theirs.[20] For now they cast Suger and spice uppon everie dish that is served
to the table: like those *Indians*, not content to weare eare-rings at the fit and
naturall place of the eares, but they will thrust Jewels through their nose and
lippes, because they will be sure to be fine.[21]

Sidney welcomes ornament; he is repelled only by its excess and mis-
placement. Moreover, the kinship of this passage to the critical sonnets reminds us that the principles of composition Sidney has in mind
are centered in the attitude of the poet himself. He must know his subject, and his style must reflect that knowledge. From this Sidney argues

[19] According to Mona Wilson, ed., *Astrophel & Stella*, p. 160, this is a reference to Ronsard and his followers.

[20] See above, Chapter 5, note 9. Sidney's estimate of Ciceronian imitation
also appears in a letter to his brother Robert, *Works*, III, 132: "So yow can
speake and write Latine not barbarously I never require great study in Ciceroni-
anisme the chiefe abuse of Oxford."

[21] *Works*, III, 42.

that a reflective style will appear artless and concludes "that acknowl-
edging our selves somewhat awry, wee may bende to the right use
both of matter and manner."[22] But his plea for restraint in the name of
sincerity and directness must not be read to favor, or even anticipate,
the subjectivity of the Romantics. Astrophel deals severely with other
styles partly to urge his own artlessness upon Stella; this is necessary
to his role as the conventional lover pleading his cause before a reluc-
tant mistress. Yet, quite apart from their dramatic purpose, his statements are nonetheless sound neoclassical doctrine. The point in these
sonnets and the point in the *Defence* is not that the poet should parade
himself or glory in his own uniqueness; he must simply tell the
truth, and the abuse of ornament is bound to inhibit this aim. Finally,
Sidney condemns not only bad and derivative stylists, but also an entire system of style, represented in prose by the imitators of Cicero and
the euphuists. He need not have been familiar with Erasmus' *Ciceronianus* to mention "*Nizolian* paper bookes," but there is little doubt that
he knew the tradition of commentary rising from that work and that
in the *Defence* and *Astrophel and Stella* its assumptions strongly color
his point of view. Ciceronianism, euphuism, and the more dangerous
tendencies of Petrarchan imitation are submitted to a common critical
standard, the paramount aim of a "plaine sensiblenesse"; or to view it
from another angle, stylistic restraint—the avoidance of obtrusive pattern, rich and exotic imagery, and derivative lyric formula—is invoked
to further the vitality of content.

If such an account of Sidney's purposes is accurate, it provokes other
questions. How closely does he follow his own rules, especially in
Astrophel and Stella? How sharp is the break between the sequence
and the carefully shaped style of the *Arcadia* poems? If he hopes to
stress the thoughtfulness of verse over the pleasures of liberal ornament, how accurately can we trace this emphasis in his own work? Are
the criteria of formal rhetoric as Sidney and his contemporaries understood them sufficient to the critical task involved? Or may they be seconded by more modern standards of evaluation?

The first two questions are raised, and I trust answered, in Chapter
6, but, to anticipate, there is no apparent decrease in the number of
rhetorical figures in *Astrophel and Stella*. Nor does Sidney hesitate to
use commonplace Petrarchan epithets and images. Many of the poems

[22] The same, III, 43.

in the sequence owe their quality simply to a more skilful use of techniques already familiar in the *Arcadia*: Sidney's fondness for amplitude and rhythmical balance survives, especially on the songs.[23] Furthermore, such a device as personification becomes, if anything, technically more central in *Astrophel and Stella*. What divides the two bodies of verse is a broad shift in Sidney's conception of the appearance of style, a change influenced, as his critical remarks suggest, by a corresponding evolution in his view of the relative importance of style and content. What we may see, as readers and as critics, are known and well-worn devices put to different and more subtle uses.

On the other hand, it might be plausible to regard the continuing presence of favored techniques in all of Sidney's work as evidence that it is unalterably founded in the same impulses. He is, after all, commonly linked with Spenser in modern criticism.[24] Both are fond of alliteration and various forms of conscious word repetition; both owe an important debt to the continental Petrarchans and to Petrarch himself; and both experiment with language and rhythm to a degree that often makes us think of them as wilfully exaggerating style over the purposes it should serve. This, at least, is the view of Yvor Winters when he brings both poets together under the charge of "decadence."[25] But this association, whether approved or deplored, is less clear-cut if we remember that Spenser's artistic tendency is always more or less towards allegory. He is fond of approaching his subject indirectly, setting it at a distance, and filtering it through the medium of elaborate conceit and sharply contoured rhythms. Sidney is rarely so committed to the "darke conceit": the sequence most of all stands distinct in this respect, and in poetic texture he falls well short of the other's deliberate artificiality.

Theodore Spencer, a friendly rather than a hostile critic, thinks of Sidney's verse as homogeneous in another way. He regards the translations of the *Psalms* and the *Arcadia* poems as exercises from which the

[23] Cf. *Astrophel and Stella*, the First, Sixth, and Seventh Songs.

[24] To some extent the identification is due to their personal association and mutual interest in exploring new possibilities for English poetic style. See C. S. Lewis, *English Literature in the Sixteenth Century Excluding Drama*, Bk. III, Chap. I. Yvor Winters, *Poetry*, LIII (1939), 324, criticizes both Sidney and Spenser for a stylistic indirection that obscures the moral force of the subject where immediacy and directness are preferable.

[25] *Poetry*, LIII (1939), 325.

mature style of *Astrophel and Stella* emerged, and he approves Sidney's ability to use strict and simple rhythms and plain diction. Like Winters he thinks of Sidney's work as generally unified in poetic aim.[26] Both views are partially correct: we can follow the traces of plain and elaborate styles through all of Sidney's lyric by using certain lines and even entire poems as touchstones. But these approaches, for all their illuminating discussion of particular lines and poems, have over-simplified the evaluation of his style. In spite of the resemblances to be found between portions of Sidney's verse, two separate principles of composition distinguish the balanced contours of the *Arcadia* poems and the comparative plainness of the sequence.

These ambiguities define Sidney's style in terms of the formal rhetoric he and his contemporaries knew, but rhetoric has its limits when we attempt to define the form of plainness which distinguishes *Astrophel and Stella*. It is true that in the sequence the figures lead more frequently to wit and understatement, where in the *Arcadia* collection, the *Psalms*, and some of the *Certaine Sonets* they cooperate with strong rhythms and emotional overstatement. And although Sidney never quite reaches the Metaphysical poets in rendering complex mental processes through the manipulation of imagery, some of his less stereotyped kinds show him bound to restraint, to the careful piecing out of ideas. These observations are well within the limits of rhetorical theory, and it is necessary to add that imagery in the view of the Renaissance is simply a phase of rhetoric. One may argue that as critics we should always treat it as such, judging Renaissance poets only by their own understanding of the strategies of language. Rosemund Tuve's insistence on this approach has helped prevent criticism from superimposing modern biases on older texts. But Renaissance assumptions about the ways in which imagery works are frequently very general, and their application may obscure very real differences between separate poems or poets. Or a poet's own statements about his art may ignore much that is obvious to us. Sidney thinks of imagery as analogical, as an adjunct to meanings which might be stated otherwise. He describes its proper use as explaining things to "a willing hearer."[27] To attempt more, according to this view, is to court redundancy. But this limitation, rising from the comparison of lyric to

---

[26] "The Poetry of Sir Philip Sidney," *ELH*, XII (1945), 251–278.
[27] *Works*, III, 42–43.

oratory, does scant justice to Sidney's ways with imagery in his own verse. His personifications in *Astrophel and Stella* seldom merely explain, and while they sharpen meaning, they do as much for the dramatic, psychological vividness and immediacy of the poems. Yet Sidney scarcely notices such effects. At most they are vaguely subsumed under the headings "delight" and "adornment": they are seen as contributing to the ardor of truth by exciting the minds of readers. Sidney's imagery, like that of any accomplished poet, is exciting; it invites the reader to join sympathetically in what he reads. But it may also add dimensions to meaning in ways that have little to do with persuasiveness (unless we allow the term to include anything that happens in a poem). The imagery of *Astrophel and Stella* discovers a particular mode of thinking which cannot be explained as relative degrees of illustrative excess or restraint.

In this respect the general question I have raised about the meaning of a distinction between poetry appealing by formal ornateness and that notable for its meditative bias needs further qualification. The classical plain style was and is justified on the grounds that it shows off truth more nakedly, subduing verbal shape in favor of plain meaning. Such a definition might well include Davies' *Nosce Teipsum* or many other didactic poems. Sidney attempts the type once or twice in the *Arcadia*.[28] But such verse is prescriptive, not dramatic or immediate: its teachings are more important than the presence of any human sensibility in the act of thinking and feeling. The lessons, if any, in *Astrophel and Stella* are important because Astrophel learns or ignores them, not because Sidney wishes to indoctrinate his readers. Yet the terms which Sidney uses to urge a plain style do not altogether encompass the difference between didactic and "thinking" verse, unless we assume that the term "lyric" makes the distinction implicitly. Certain modes of formal rhetoric and logic do contribute to the greater "sententious density" of the sequence, but its sonnets offer more than meditative depth and clarity. For this reason it is necessary to extend our view of what Sidney accomplishes through various levels of language; the precepts by which he explicitly sanctions certain modes of rhythm, figure, or trope are not enough, for they fail to predict the

[28] See "As I my little flocke on Ister banke" (*Works*, I, 132), "A neighbor mine not long ago there was" (the same, II, 66), "Since natures workes be good, and death doth serve" (the same, II, 166).

end result of his style. *Astrophel and Stella* defines itself as the dramatic, immediate expression of a mind in the act of thinking and feeling; the verse is psychologically vital and internally revealing, whatever the burden of conventional ornament and attitude it is forced to bear. Behind the style of the sequence there is a spirit meditating, questioning, arguing, exulting and complaining; above all it is a spirit driven by skepticism. We must look here for the immediate organizing principle of Sidney's "plain" style. To do so we need advance no new categories of technique which Sidney ignored in his own work or critical theory, but we must enlarge the conception of the goals to which familiar techniques are directed.

6.

The Structures of Energetic Style

$\mathcal{N}$early every critic who has written about *Astrophel and Stella* has had to grapple with its confusing mixture of conventionality and freshness, its apparently haphazard· lumping together of Petrarchan clichés and arresting ironies. Nearly every critic has felt compelled to choose sides and promote whichever element he thinks most characteristic. Perhaps the truth is that the mixture itself is definitive of Sidney's most mature work, for it is difficult not to recognize the most obvious tradition consorting with something new and strong in his expression. Sidney anticipates both the fervid analysis of emotion of Shakespeare's sonnets and the neat, dramatic voice of Herbert's varied lyrics.

Yet the variety of *Astrophel and Stella* may seem paradoxical. The translations of the *Psalms,* the *Certaine Sonets,* and the *Arcadia* poems are far more eclectic in verse form, line length, stanzaic pattern, and lyric type. In the sequence Sidney concentrates almost exclusively on the sonnet (there are eleven songs), and he writes exclusively about love. (Even Petrarch had varied his matter with addresses to friends, comments on politics and other issues.) But the uniformity is only apparent: rhythm and tone are subject to quick, often bewildering shifts at different points in the sequence; and they may even change within a single poem. The sort of stylistic continuity we noted in the *Arcadia* is absent here, and that absence is crucial.

To say this much is not to deny *Astrophel and Stella* its coherence. But what makes it a unified work of art lies deeper than a simple preference for one kind of rhythm or figure or verse form. In spite of one or two inconsistencies, *Astrophel and Stella* has a continuous narrative thread, and it is controlled by one sensibility. Even more important, the shifts and changes in mood and style can be drawn together under purposes consistent with each other, and on these terms it can be set apart from the rest of Sidney's verse.[1]

Some of these purposes have already been touched upon. Sidney's explicit preference for informal, plain, "sententious" lyric grows out of his concern for the persuasiveness of a style which appears to have shed the more obvious and trite means to ornament. And, if we look back at most of the *Arcadia* verse, we recall that it is a collection of set pieces, embellishing the prose narrative. The *Arcadia* poems assume an attitude towards the expression of feeling that is almost ritualistic, not unlike the style of the early plays of Shakespeare, and with such an assumption it is natural that formal symmetries should control the discourse. The narrative base of the sequence and its tendency to debate and argue the sensations it expresses foster a style more flexible and casual, one that handles emotion with less fanfare but makes it ultimately more interesting. The fixed moods of Sidney's decorative verse give way to states of feeling in swift, often surprising movement. Astrophel may speak formally and conventionally: he exhibits most of the standard poses of the stereotyped lover, but the exhibition is self-conscious and it is complicated by other ways of regarding love and expressing it.

All this is to say that *Astrophel and Stella* is a more lively and living kind of poetry, and the difference is at once apparent in the way Sidney handles formal and casual rhythms in the same poem:

> She comes, and streight therewith her shining twins do move,
>> Their rayes to me, who in her tedious absence lay
>> Benighted in cold wo, but now appeares my day,
>> The onely light of joy, the only warmth of *Love.*

[1] The most exhaustive and convincing analysis of the unity of the sequence is Richard B. Young's *English Petrarke: A Study of Sidney's Astrophel and Stella*; see below, Chapter 7.

She comes with light and warmth, which like *Aurora* prove
  Of gentle force, so that mine eyes dare gladly play
  With such a rosie morne, whose beames most freshly gay
  Scortch not, but onely do darke chilling sprites remove.

But lo, while I do speake, it groweth noone with me,
  Her flamie glistring lights increase with time and place;
  My heart cries ah, it burnes, mine eyes now dazled be:

No wind, no shade can coole, what helpe then in my case,
  But with short breath, long lookes, staid feet and walking hed,
  Pray that my sunne go downe with meeker beames to bed.
                                    (Sonnet 76)

Like its companion piece, Sonnet 77, this poem invokes the rhythms, language, and tone of Petrarchan adulation for its own destruction. The surprising outcome is not entirely facetious: one of the major themes of the sequence is the contradiction of idealistic emotion by sexual desire. The hyperbole and amplitude of the Petrarchan manner last until the final tercet; at that point the imagery becomes immediate and dramatic, preparing for the extension of the conceit that Stella is the sun a step beyond the reader's expectation.

There is no apparent clash of stately and plain rhythms in Sonnet 77, but in every other respect it epitomizes Sidney's habit of sharply modifying the conventional style of love to bring it up against the realities of feeling. In Sonnet 76 these realities are mostly translated by imagery ("wind," "shade," "short breath," "long lookes, staid feet and walking hed"), but Sidney is equally capable of similar effects by means of the speaking voice, relaxed rhythms, and blunt statements.

The last line of Sonnet 1, "Foole, said my Muse to me, looke in thy heart and write," remains the most famous of Sidney's direct, almost dramatic outbursts. Nothing like it exists in the *Arcadia* poems,[2] but there are many parallels in *Astrophel and Stella*. The ending of Sonnet 19, "Scholler, saith *Love*, bend hitherward your wit," uses exactly the same construction, and in Sonnet 21 direct address occupies the entire final tercet:

[2] The pastoral, "A Shepheards tale no height of stile desires" (*Works*, II, 214), attempts the "low" style, but its plainness consists in the use of imagery to reflect a rustic environment. Otherwise, the poem is every bit as ornamental as the rest of the *Arcadia* verse.

> Sure you say well, your wisdomes golden mine,
>> Dig deepe with learnings spade, now tell me this,
>> Hath this world ought so faire as *Stella* is?

There is little apparent contour to this verse; none of the tight balance so familiar in Sidney's ornate work remains; the speaking voice seems to create its own order and its own emphasis.

But the vocal qualities of *Astrophel and Stella* are usually involved in wit, and when they are, Sidney characteristically turns to figures of repetition for his context. Often the repetition is a form of word play, as in Sonnet 5: "True, and yet true that I must *Stella* love," or the audacious ending to Sonnet 92, "Say all, and all, well sayd, still say the same." Antithesis finishes off a number of sonnets: "Such light in sense, with such a darkned mind" (Sonnet 99). These examples are typical, not exhaustive, but, more important, they remind us that much of the freshness and energy of the sequence is managed without any real lessening of the number of formal rhetorical devices. They are simply used with more discretion. The instances just noted use rhetoric not for its own sake but for the sake of the wit—twenty-eight sonnets are so concluded—and only rarely can we accuse Sidney of reaching beyond the immediate purposes of the poem to indulge in rhetorical virtuosity.[3]

Although continually mixed with various degrees of formal speech, the colloquialism of *Astrophel and Stella* imposes a distinctive texture on the discourse, and it is a point of reference for a number of elements in Sidney's "plainness." Wit is one of these, and wit naturally leads us to consider more closely what Sidney calls the "sententious density" of poetic style. Besides the use of rhythmical balance to set off antithesis or word play, he favors devices which move away from symmetry to the appearance of a casual irregularity. Sonnets 47 and 74 both use a line broken by strong pauses at irregular intervals, but Sonnet 34 goes even further to give a meditative structure the semblance of vocal spontaneity:

> Come let me write, and to what end? to ease
>> A burthned hart, how can words ease, which are
>> The glasses of thy dayly vexing care?
>> Oft cruell fights well pictured forth do please.

[3] See Sonnet 9 which uses the figure syllepsis in its bewildering conclusion.

Art not asham'd to publish thy disease?
>Nay, that may breed my fame, it is so rare:
>But will not wise men thinke thy words fond ware?
>Then be they close, and so none shall displease.

What idler thing, then speake and not be hard?
>What harder thing then smart, and not to speake?
>Peace foolish wit, with wit my wit is mard.

Thus write I while I doubt to write, and wreake
>My harmes on Inks poore losse, perhaps some find
>*Stellas* great powrs, that so confuse my mind.

The form is governed by an old convention (that used in medieval debates between the body and the soul), but the use of two speakers to represent inner debate is none the less convincing. Stylistically, the sonnet divides after line eleven where the dialogue ceases and Astrophel explains and sums up the condition he has tried to expose dramatically. The change in voice forces some increase in formality, and line twelve has two figures of repetition. But the figures are not responsible for transforming the style, for the heaviest frequency of rhetorical devices occurs earlier in the sonnet.[4] Instead the style owes much of its freshness to the quietness of the figures. There is full freedom in the vocal pattern.

Sonnet 34 is at once thoughtful, psychologically accurate, wryly humorous ("Peace foolish wit, with wit my wit is mard"), and perfectly controlled. It seems to present Astrophel's mind to us debating an urgent problem and unencumbered by the poet's strategies. Under the microscope the sonnet has a definite, observable structure, but it is a structure perfectly apt to suggest a mind in the act of thinking and feeling. Because Sidney betrays no need to cultivate symmetry, he is able to use "ornament" efficiently and naturally and here at least he is convincing without the orator's habit of repeating for emphasis.

The vocal freedom of the sequence, with its seemingly unpremeditated order, should be measured against the *Arcadia* poems, especially where the latter make an attempt at serious thoughtfulness.

---

[4] Miss Rubel, *Poetic Diction in the English Renaissance,* p. 206, lists anthypophora as the dominant figure. Lines nine through eleven also contain ploce and prosonomasia.

One of the pastoral entertainments at the end of the third book of the *Arcadia* is a debate between Reason and Passion, and it is instructive to see how differently it manages the development of contesting ideas:

> Reason. Thou Rebell vile, come, to thy master yelde.
> Passion. No, Tyrant, no: mine, mine shall be the fielde.
> R.   Can *Reason* then a Tyraunt counted be?
> P.   If *Reason* will, that *Passions* be not free.
> R.   But *Reason* will, that *Reason* governe most.
> P.   And *Passion* will, that *Passion* rule the rost.
> R.   Your will is will; but *Reason* reason is.
> P.   Will hath his will, when *Reasons* will doth misse.
> R.   Whom *Passion* leades unto his death is bent.
> P.   And let him die, so that he died content.
> R.   By nature you to *Reason* faith have sworne.
> P.   Not so, but fellowlike together borne.
> R.   Who *Passion* doth ensue, lives in annoy.
> P.   Who *Passion* doth forsake, lives void of joy.
> R.   *Passion* is blinde, and treades an unknowne trace.
> P.   *Reason* hath eyes to see his owne ill case.
>
> (*Works*, I, 339)

The verse moves on through the same persistent, self-contained couplets endlessly poising Reason and Passion (or more properly right reason and sophistry) against each other. The method is inexorable and self-defeating: the rhythm is monotonously balanced; the sentence units are uniformly brief; the double meanings are efficient but predictable. Sidney introduces the piece as a "daūce, which they called the skirmish betwixt *Reason* and *Passion*," inadvertently putting his finger on what is wrong with the poem. The dancing measure, intended to imitate the alternate thrusts of the opposing personifications, amounts to an exaggeration of form which hamstrings the play of the ideas. The poem is academic and arty, precisely the qualities Sidney thought hostile to a "sound stile":

Undoubtedly (at least to my opinion undoubtedly) I have found in divers smal learned Courtiers, a more sound stile, then in some professors of learning of which I can gesse no other cause, but that the Courtier following that which by practise he findeth fittest to nature, therein (though he know it not) doth according to art, thogh not by art: where the other using art to shew art and not hide art (as in these cases he shuld do) flieth from nature, & indeed abuseth art.[5]

In a similar fashion, the apparent ease and artlessness of many (but by no means all) of the sonnets, conceal the most complex art. Sidney perfects one kind of style in the *Arcadia* poems, and it is verbally and rhythmically elaborate but tends to monotony. By repeating a clear, sharp symmetry through various stages of his medium he achieves his best decorative effects. In *Astrophel and Stella* poetic form is apt to move away from symmetry, to assume different, changing, and un-expected shapes, even within a single poem. This flexibility seems less ornamental, more natural in the way it handles the speakers' sensations. A different concept of imitation is at work in the sequence. The style is not uniformly colloquial any more than it is uniformly oratorical. It uses figures of repetition and amplitude, but it seldom lets the impulse to repeat govern the strategy of the poem. It is capable of wit, even to excess, but wit never becomes a mannerism or the main purpose for which the verse is written. Yet at the same time Sidney's variety stays clear of technical chaos and allows him to use shifting orders of rhythm and rhetoric for different purposes. He can be facetious as in Sonnet 17, while he endows myth with dramatic urgency; he can manage an ironic tone even as he recounts the poignancy of Astrophel's falling in love (Sonnet 2); or he can render the most wistful melan-choly sliding into the bitterest reproach (Sonnet 31). Each of these is fairly representative of the larger modes of expression in the sequence; yet each one of them must be thought of as a set of related and de-veloping ideas, their complexity of thought enhanced by Sidney's lessened interest in symmetry as its own excuse. Thus, the greater thoughtfulness of the sequence is everywhere translated by flexibility of technique. Sonnet 1 demonstrates that this can be so without any loss in continuity, and it is typical of Sidney's best procedure elsewhere:

> Loving in truth, and faine in verse my love to show,
> That she (deare she) might take some pleasure of my paine:
> Pleasure might cause her reade, reading might make her know,
> Knowledge might pitie winne, and pitie grace obtaine,

[5] *Works*, II, 43.

> I sought fit words to paint the blackest face of woe,
>> Studying inventions fine, her wits to entertaine:
>> Oft turning others leaves, to see if thence would flow
>> Some fresh and fruitfull showers upon my sunne-burn'd braine.
>
> But words came halting forth, wanting Inventions stay,
>> Invention Natures child, fled step-dame Studies blowes,
>> And others feete still seem'd but strangers in my way.
>
> Thus great with child to speake, and helplesse in my throwes,
>> Biting my trewand pen, beating my selfe for spite,
>> Foole, said my Muse to me, looke in thy heart and write.

Sonnet 1 is especially interesting because it manages such a neat adjustment between balanced and varied discourse. Sidney uses the figure climax[6] twice, in the first quatrain and again in lines nine and ten. Climax shapes and relates ideas in a narrative order with mounting emphasis, and in most cases the alexandrines have the caesura after the third foot, evenly splitting the line. Furthermore, the total movement of the poem is narrative, leading from the motive of desire through the frustrated attempt to write imitative, bookish verse to the discovery of the proper source of invention in the self. The key line is the last, but this is only the greatest in a series of four climaxes, each slightly different. The first three are neatly fitted to the two quatrains and the first tercet. In addition the sonnet has the quality of an action complete in itself and fully motivated. This action, involving a change in attitude, is basic to the structure of the lines. By contrast, the rhythm is incidental, nor is it so thoroughly balanced as the evenly divided lines would suggest. For instance, the first quatrain moves towards a balanced symmetry: lines one and two split after the second foot, while lines three and four, where climax becomes most obvious in the parallel structure of the phrases, are evenly halved. But in the second quatrain the first caesura is very light and occurs after the second foot. Lines six and seven are nearly parallel in structure, but line eight, extending the account of Astrophel's purpose, immediately destroys the balance. Then Sidney returns once more to symmetrically proportioned lines, a pair of them, in the first tercet, but shifts again in line eleven, stressing the completion of the trope: "And others

[6] See Appendix A.

84

feete still seem'd but strangers in my way." Finally, the conclusion of the sonnet picks up the symmetry a last time in lines twelve and thirteen only to contradict them with a line of two pauses, both strong.

The essential rhythm of Sonnet 1 is thus cyclical rather than consistently balanced. Sidney forces it to conform to the stages of the narrative, using it to prepare for key statements but muting it for the statements themselves. This repeated approach to and withdrawal from an even rhythmical contour forms a pattern of its own, but it is not rigid. The rhythmical sequence of the first quatrain (Sidney obviously wishes only a tempered climax in "and pitie grace obtaine") differs from that of the second, and at the end of the sonnet Sidney abandons his narrative and rhetorical strategy to get his most telling effect through the blunt force of direct speech. He is working here with a serving, rather than a commanding, rhythm, allotting symmetry only so much prominence as is useful for other purposes.

What is evident in the opening statement of *Astrophel and Stella* governs, to a greater or lesser degree, the majority of its poems. For the sake of direct contact between the mind of Astrophel and that of the reader and for the sake of careful blocking out of Astrophel's thinking, Sidney has adopted a plastic style, shifting from formality to spontaneity, balance to variety, rhetorical amplitude to understatement or the conciseness of wit. And there is an analogy to these procedures in the total scheme of the sequence. It is, to repeat, compounded of several styles. The first two sonnets are narrative and introductory. Then Sidney alternates, until Sonnet 30, between obviously conventional renderings of Astrophel's devotion (poems of praise and complaint) and his rigorous moral inquiry into his own motives. The sonnets in praise of Stella (their tone is repeated and intensified later in such poems as Sonnets 42, 43, and 48) are most reminiscent of the love lyrics in the *Arcadia*. The formulas of eulogy and the rounded balance of the lines are only partially modified by Sidney's wit. Sonnet 31 strikes a mode almost evenly informed by rhetorical balance and repetition on the one hand and the urgency of the living, questioning voice of Astrophel on the other. Sonnet 34 and several following it demonstrate Sidney's plainer mode (in reality a manner never entirely absent at any stage of the sequence), while those poems devoted to Astrophel's sexual pursuit of his mistress (Sonnets 66, 67, 68, 69, 70, 77, and Sonnets 79, 80, 81, the "kiss" sonnets) revive the ornate amplitude of strong emotional sensations. There is no set pattern to the occurrence of these styles; the effect of their varied appearance, reappearance, and intermixture is to give us what C. S. Lewis calls an "anatomy of love,"[7] an imitation of the varied moods and mental operations of a poet-lover, introspective, despairing, confident, adoring, reproachful, jealous, angry, joyous, or resigned. It is axiomatic that for all of these no single mode of expression would be adequate, and it is particularly certain that the stylized consistency of the *Arcadia* verse would be a disaster. Yet in its place ornateness is appropriate. Most of the eleven songs in *Astrophel and Stella* are rhythmically and rhetorically more heavily patterned than the rest of the sequence. One or two (the narrative Fourth and Eighth Songs) are relatively plain, but most of the others exploit all the resources of balance and fulness of expression. Like the *Arcadia* lyrics they are set pieces, abstracting emotions from the main flow of the sequence and giving them a more emphatic and extended voice.

> Doubt you to whom my Muse these notes entendeth,
> Which now my breast orecharg'd to Musicke lendeth?
> To you, to you, all song of praise is due,
> Only in you my song begins and endeth.
>
> (First Song)

It is clear enough that *Astrophel and Stella* is a tissue of shifting moods and states of mind, a kaleidoscope of the lover's sensations. What is less clear is the persistence of Astrophel's need to look into himself, to assess the ground he stands on, to question and establish the geography of his emotions. To a degree Sonnet 1 with its carefully pieced out stages of narrative leading to a decision illuminates the meditative bent of Astrophel's mind. Sonnet 34 is even more definite in establishing the rhythmical and rhetorical texture of his debate with himself, and this introspective procedure is almost habitual if we consider how many poems it controls.[8] It most nearly translates for us what Sidney means in the *Defence* when he speaks of the "sententious density of the matter." But the accompaniment of a shifting, vocal tempo, the ironic juxtaposition of ornate and plain statements, or the

---

[7] *English Literature in the Sixteenth Century Excluding Drama*, p. 329.
[8] See below, Chap. 7.

interrogative order of debate are seconded by Sidney's use of imagery. Through it we may observe the energy of his logic, and in his distinctive use of personification an ease in joining precision and vitality of statement, to give a further dramatic focus to the voice of Astrophel.

The conceits of the *Arcadia* verse gravitate either towards Petrarchan formula or towards the correct but labored use of imagery for logical embellishment. The following is clear and correct, but its very exactness robs the verse of life and feeling:

> My sheepe are thoughts, which I both guide and serve:
> Their pasture is faire hilles of fruitlesse Love:
> On barren sweetes they feede, and feeding sterve:
> I waile their lotte, but will not other prove.
>
> (*Works*, I, 163)

After the initial statement of likeness, the images appear to carry the discourse, but their success depends entirely upon the reader's ability to hold the separate notions of sheep and thoughts and the speaker's relation to both of them distinct. Several standard logical predicaments are exploited one after the other—"manner of doing," "where," "manner of suffering," and "manner of doing" a second time.[9] The passage is mildly complicated by more than one set of parallels, but each is obvious. The imagery remains an embellishment, convenient for vivifying the idea contained in the phrase, "which I both guide and serve." But the rather primitive kind of vivification we find here is essentially the illustrative maneuver of the orator. The logic is too openly managed; Sidney fastens the conceit on his subject and allows it to smother any sense of action the lines might conceivably develop.

Such procedure is typical of ornate sixteenth century verse. Spenser's imagery in *Amoretti* frequently transforms lyric into something like epic simile; he is even fonder than Sidney of elaborate but static conceits, fully developed and symmetrically rounded off. [10] The same esthetic principles underlie Sidney's use of the pathetic fallacy in the *Arcadia*: he is inclined to animate nature (or parts of the human body) as a springboard for illustration or explanation, as in "Locke up, faire

---

[9] Rosemund Tuve, *Elizabethan and Metaphysical Imagery*, is a useful reference for these matters; see esp. p. 285.

[10] See, for example, Spenser's Sonnet 18, "The rolling wheele that runneth often round."

liddes, the treasure of my harte" (*Works*, II, 26) or "Do not disdaine, ô streight up raised Pine" (the same, II, 24). The latter exploits the lover's carving of his initials in the tree to discuss the wounds of love in the heart, a parallel open to Sidney's own charge that ornate verse unnecessarily duplicates "similitudes." Moreover, such mannered conceits too openly proclaim their mechanics because Sidney concentrates too intently on their expository uses, slighting the dramatic power of imagery controlled by the casual speaking voice.

Rosemund Tuve, in her treatment of the logical functions of Renaissance imagery, has been especially concerned with the Elizabethan tendency to dwell on elementary logical comparisons, and she differentiates it from later practice in these terms:

Puzzling differences of effect between "Elizabethan" and "Metaphysical" conceits are often explicable as differences between extended pursuit of a simple logical parallel and extended pursuit of a likeness by basing it on several logical parallels.[11]

The "extended pursuit of a simple logical parallel" governs the development of the following lines, which announce rather blatantly the fact that a formal comparison is being made:

> Like divers flowers, whose divers beauties serve
> To decke the earth with his well-colourde weede,
> Though each of them, his private forme preserve,
> Yet joyning formes one sight of beautie breede.
>
> Right so my thoughts, where on my hart I feede:
> Right so my inwarde partes, and outward glasse,
> Though each possesse a divers working kinde,
> Yet all well knit to one faire end do passe:
>   That he to whome, these sondrie giftes I binde
>   All what I am, still one, his owne, doe finde.
> (Works, II, 26)

Sidney's careful separation of tenor and vehicle implies more than neatness: the tenor ("Right so my thoughts . . . ") needs no simile to clarify it. Like the poem cited earlier this is clearly decorative. And in support of Miss Tuve's contention, the parallel is based entirely on

[11] *Elizabethan and Metaphysical Imagery*, p. 294.

"manner of doing": in spite of the detail employed, the logic is simple and transparent.

Perhaps the most important feature in this example is the absence of any personal voice in the first four lines, and when we turn from the *Arcadia* poems to *Astrophel and Stella*, it is the voice of the protagonist which transforms and animates the imagery, just as it releases and reshapes the rhythm. Sometimes Astrophel's tongue (or Sidney's pen) seems to falter; sometimes it seems to lose its identity in the mazes of conventional Petrarchan epithet ("O eyes, which do the Spheares of beautie move"); sometimes it retreats before the relentless elaboration of a difficult conceit (for example, Sonnet 49: "I on my horse, and *Love* on me, doth trie"). But when Sidney evades such dangers, *Astrophel and Stella* demonstrates a fusion of logic and psychological directness difficult to find elsewhere in his work. In this context, precision and vitality rise from the personal voice (symbolic of the mind) fashioning imagery to logical purposes.

Yet the imagery itself may create a living world because it can suggest human action, not by explanation, but by offering a background of movement, gesture, and sensation. Sonnet 18 has an energy which may be explained partly by vocal tonalities and the kind of flexible structure of discourse we have already noted, but mainly by the fact that the imagery is driven towards physical movement.

> With what sharpe checkes I in my selfe am shent,
> > When into Reasons audite I do go:
> > And by just counts my selfe a banckrout know
> > Of all those goods, which heav'n to me have lent:
>
> Unable quite to pay even Natures rent,
> > Which unto it by birthright I do ow:
> > And which is worse, no good excuse can show,
> > But that my wealth I have most idly spent.
>
> My youth doth waste, my knowledge brings forth toyes,
> > My wit doth strive those passions to defend,
> > Which for reward spoile it with vaine annoyes.
>
> I see my course to loose my selfe doth bend:
> > I see and yet no greater sorow take,
> > Then that I loose no more for *Stellas* sake.

Sonnet 18 is logically, not verbally, formal; or more precisely its logical structure is most in evidence and helps control and direct the thoughtful tone fitting to introspection of this kind. The controlling image is the familiar one of casting one's accounts, gain and loss being used by Astrophel to gauge his intellectual and moral failure. This image draws everything to itself and at the same time it is pursued systematically through all fourteen lines. Unlike the strained parallels of Sonnet 49 (where at one point Astrophel is led to remark, "A horseman to my horse, a horse to *Love*"), each stage of the comparison here develops easily out of the last. Accounting is succeeded by the recognition of bankruptcy, which in turn gives way to the slight tautology, an inability to pay. Then Astrophel acknowledges his lack of valid excuse and next his continued prodigality, which continues because its cause persists. The final tercet reaches still further: Astrophel sees that he risks a loss of "selfe" and sees also that he does not mind. Lifted out of its conventional moral context, improvidence becomes almost a virtue: "I see and yet no greater sorow take / Then that I loose no more for *Stellas* sake." Moreover a series of strong verbs, suggestive of physical movement and energy, accompany the logical development of the trope: "shent," "waste," "brings forth," "strive," "defend," "spoile," "bend." These are in no sense remarkable; they are commonplace, unobtrusive words, but Sidney concentrates them toward the movement of emotional crisis just before the grouping controlled by the repeated "I see." Logical method and verbal strength are kept in judicious balance, and the sonnet is effective because Sidney is able quietly to mix systematic meditation, a valid psychological sequence (the movement of Astrophel's mind from the initial impulse to self-assessment to confession of guilt, which lasts in spite of confession, to the final assertion that his error is worthwhile), and dramatic, mildly witty surprise without strain or appearance of artifice.

Few of the sonnets are logically more intricate than this, but several are psychologically and emotionally as direct, and in contemplating them we must add to vocal rhythm and logical neatness Sidney's habit of personification. The intentional, rather open fantasy with which this device is used in the *Arcadia*, conceit parading as conceit, survives only once or twice in the sequence. In Sonnet 84, "High way, since you my chiefe *Pernassus* be," or in Sonnet 103, "O happie Tems, that didst my *Stella* beare," personification is nearly ludicrous. Instead of opening a way into the mind of the speaker and fostering the lively meditation which the dramatic force of implied dialogue may give, these sonnets are tyrannized by the conceit. The taint of artificiality also colors some of the early sonnets. Several of these dramatize myth as a form of praise and declaration of love. A brief narration of Cupid's search for a home (Sonnet 8) is manipulated so that Astrophel may approach Stella's cold beauty and his own ardor from an extreme esthetic distance, isolating emotion from immediate circumstance. Sonnets 11, 12, 13, and 17 are precisely similar, and if, as a recent critic says, they are useful, it is to fix Astrophel's role in the early moments of the sequence as the traditional Petrarchan lover.[12]

With personification Sidney is most effective when he relieves it of its burden of fantasy. J. W. Lever rightly understands Sidney's use of it as dramatic, giving Astrophel the chance to talk, from time to time, to the animated and contending elements in his own mind. He also notes that a further effect is to make Astrophel's the only fully articulated personality in the sequence.[13] Astrophel also addresses Stella, one or two friends, "envious wits," and the like. Most obviously, of course, the resultant variety keeps the discourse moving and flexible. Personification cooperates in this respect with Sidney's use of free vocal tempo, sudden wit, and energetic imagery to strengthen the vitality and directness of his style. But his achievement here is neither new nor surprising. Petrarch had done it before him, just as Petrarch had established the introspective formulas of amorous verse. Where Sidney differs, I think, is in his ability to depart from personification merely as conceit, which tends through its formality to fix a distance between the subject and the mind of the speaker dwelling on the subject. Personification as conceit need have no narrative context (although it clearly does in the mythological poems early in the sequence); the highway and the "Tems" of Sonnets 84 and 103 are merely silent partners in dialogue with Astrophel. But Sidney's most frequent maneuver in implied or open dialogue is to personify abstractions, rather than natural objects or mythological figures.

More important than the origin of these devices is the manner in which Sidney makes them work. Several times his personifications

---

[12] Richard B. Young, *English Petrarke: A Study of Sidney's Astrophel and Stella*; see esp. p. 40.

[13] *The Elizabethan Love Sonnet*, pp. 84–85, 88.

appear suddenly and dramatically, coinciding with a shift in rhythm and rhetorical strategy. The opening of Sonnet 71 is soberly expository and briefly impersonal:

> Who will in fairest booke of Nature know,
>> How Vertue may best lodg'd in beautie be,
>> Let him but learne of *Love* to reade in thee
>> *Stella,* those faire lines, which true goodnesse show.

Thus far the personifications, virtue and beauty, have no dramatic role, no voice. Following the didactic tone of the first three lines, Astrophel's direct address to Stella is a surprise, emphasized by the position of "thee" and the enjambment of the third and fourth lines. But the second quatrain returns at first to formal oratory:

> There shall he find all vices overthrow,
>> Not by rude force, but sweetest soveraigntie
>> Of reason, from whose light those night-birds flie;
>> That inward sunne in thine eyes shineth so.

Yet these lines are not so inert. Sidney has begun to complicate the imagery, building the images of warfare and rule and flight within the initial conceit that Stella's beauty is a text to be read with profit. The activity implied in these lines compensates for the muting of the living voice, and the vital presence of Stella moves more into the foreground in the next passage:

> And not content to be Perfections heire
>> Thy selfe, doest strive all minds that way to move:
>> Who marke in thee what is in thee most faire.

Yet the style remains largely expository and continues so for two more lines:

> So while thy beautie drawes the heart to love,
>> As fast thy Vertue bends that love to good:
>
> But ah, Desire still cries, give me some food.

I have isolated the last line because it isolates itself. The poem is built

92

on the same principle as Sonnet 1. With the sudden shift in values (from the carefully virtuous to the sexually and subjectively impetuous) Sidney interposes direct speech and blunt, coarse metaphor.

Such a change in the final line is not usual in the sonnet. The Italian form, of which Sidney uses various modifications, commonly divides at the octave, but this division need only be superficial. The sonnet is a kind of verse paragraph, encouraging singleness of tone and a predictable and uniform development of idea. Sidney's means of escaping a commonplace structure are several. We have seen that he often achieves surprise or wit through word play or rhetorical antithesis.[14] Sonnets 1 and 71 typify another means of conquering the appearance of formality and developing the sonnet as an ironic instrument. Moreover, his freedom from stereotyped technique is an excellent means for imitating the emerging (in Sonnet 1) or continuing (in Sonnet 71) vitality of impulses apparently destroyed by Astrophel's failure to write and by his submission to the stylized role of the virtuous lover. These poems are the battleground for the emotional struggles of the protagonist, and his changing and complicated allegiance to one impulse or the other finds its mirror in Sidney's way with plain and fancy styles. The modes of personification and the modes of discourse surrounding and containing them epitomize his tact in varying from the formal to the casual or abrupt to keep his medium in step with the changing and contrary mind of Astrophel.

More frequently the personifications work through entire sonnets as actors in the discourse. An abstraction that can be spoken to has a vastly different role than one evoked simply in narration or exposition. Astrophel talks to and within himself when he addresses "Vertue" (Sonnet 4), "Reason" (Sonnet 10), "School of patience" (Sonnet 56), "Hope" (Sonnet 67), "Desire" (Sonnet 72), "Griefe" (Sonnet 94), or "Thought" (Sonnet 96). These represent only a fraction of the poems in which Sidney gives life to the abstract or inanimate (the moon, a bed, or the "Tems")—there are forty-two poems, including the Second, Third, Ninth, and Tenth Songs, of this character—but they exemplify those pieces in which the style approaches the inflections of casual speech. Some, of course, are more nearly formal or

---

[14] This strategy is habitual; see the conclusions of Sonnets 5, 10, 14, 16, 35, 54, 57, 58, 60, 61, 62, 63, 64, 65, 67, 78, 79, 80, 82, 86, 87, 91, 92, 93, 96, 99, 101, 108.·

oratorical, but the general effect is dramatic, vivifying the personality of Astrophel responding to the world around and within him.

The poems in which personifications are alive become all the more significant for the general tone of the sequence when they are put beside those in which Astrophel speaks to other human beings—most often, of course, to Stella. Sonnets 4 and 10 (addressed to "Vertue" and "Reason") are scarcely different in subject or texture from Sonnet 14, directed to "my friend," and Astrophel also talks to other friends, poets, "Lordings," a sparrow, and "envious wits." This group totals forty-one sonnets, and the two groups between them comprise roughly two-thirds of the sequence. The result is not, as one might suppose, to divide Astrophel's private meditations from his external relations with Stella and others. Rather both modes of existence seem to move on the same level and intermingle. Personification is essentially a deliberate fantasy undertaken by the poet, but Sidney deprives it of its fantastic clothing and domesticates it to the world of speech and gesture.

No other element of Sidney's style is so surely responsible for the energy of *Astrophel and Stella*. With few exceptions, his followers grasped only the formulas of amorous praise and complaint and brought the sonnet sequence into disrepute in a very short time, but his real achievement was difficult to imitate. He found the means to create a living mind in a living present by mingling varied speech forms and the familiarity with which his personifications—his "actors"—move. But at the same time this manner stays well within the limits imposed by Sidney's attention to the rigors of meditative organization. Few of the sonnets lack a basic logical pattern, and in some it is both intricate and precise. Again and again they reach conclusions on the basis of evidence, or search for causes and effects, or argue opposing values, or call upon likenesses to strengthen an assertion or reinforce a plea. *Astrophel and Stella* is thus doubly vigorous, able to respond in varying degrees of dramatic or logical energy. This can be demonstrated even in a poem not notable for its vocal informality and yet unhampered by obvious Arcadian symmetry:

> Griefe find the words, for thou hast made my braine
> So darke with misty vapors, which arise
> From out thy heavy mould, that inbent eyes
> Can scarce discerne the shape of mine owne paine.

Do thou then (for thou canst) do thou complaine,
   For my poore soule, which now that sicknesse tries,
   Which even to sence, sence of its selfe denies,
   Though harbengers of death lodge there his traine.

Or if thy love of plaint yet mine forbeares,
   As of a caitife worthy so to die,
   Yet waile thy selfe, and waile with causefull teares,

That though in wretchednesse thy life doth lie,
   Yet growest more wretched then thy nature beares,
   By being placed in such a wretch as I.
                   (Sonnet 94)

What makes this sonnet stand halfway between formal and informal (or ornamental and plain) style is best seen in relation to the personification of grief. Astrophel has attempted Stella's seduction and failed for the last time; all his reserves of ascendent desire have been exhausted (see the Tenth Song and Sonnet 93). The effect of his address, like his earlier addresses to Cupid, is to link his despair with an abstract, universal condition. A more immediate result is the conceit that grief is outdone by the extremity of Astrophel's private distress, but this is not to remove human sensation to the level of the strange or fantastic. The poem shares in Sidney's habit of definition by witty indirection. But the style is subtler than this.

What is striking is its fusion of apparent continuity with a neatly sectioned grouping of ideas. It moves from Astrophel's remark that he cannot look searchingly within himself, to an acknowledgment of his soul's danger, transparently disguised as an appeal to grief to plead for him. The portents of this direction of thought find some relief in the sestet: grief itself may suffer beyond his proper measure "by being placed in such a wretch as I." The conceit is deliberately transparent; through the personification which allows conceited statement, Astrophel continues to explore and define his own condition. His address to grief supplies tonal continuity and a framework for analysis: here, as in Astrophel's remarks to the moon (Sonnet 31), Sidney's manner appears to be not so much an ornamental, stylized indirection as a slight objective distance, a drawing back from the self for careful measurement. For the last stage of the sonnet carries beyond clever hyperbole to imply that Astrophel's own grief is excessive. Early in the piece he "could scarce discerne the shape of mine owne paine," but at the end he has discerned it very well and touched on its source ("that sicknesse") and its effects (a blurring of the senses). Valued for its surface texture alone, Sonnet 94 is merely Astrophel's rather conventional testimony to the strength of his grief; beneath the surface it is a striking piece of self-criticism, his recognition that he grieves more than he should. At the last line he has moved outside self-pity, beyond the need of an advocate to "complaine" for his "poore soule," to the knowledge that he is wretched because his despair exceeds normal limits.

The end product, therefore, is a verse that seeks to know as well as to express, a mode of discernment aided and enhanced by personification. Direct, casual speech is largely muted in Sonnet 94, although line five—"Do thou then (for thou canst) do thou complaine"—hints at it. However, its faintness is not the result of an attempt at formal symmetry but rather of the prominence of meditative exactness. The vocal tonality is just strong enough to bear the presence of a single sensibility divided in two for its own understanding.

It is clear by now that "plaine sensiblenesse" has relative and shifting proportions in Sidney's style. If such a broad term is at all capable of definition—both by standards of traditional rhetorical thinking and those implied by Yvor Winters' criteria of directness and immediacy— it is best described by Sidney's ability to modulate his style for a variety of purposes. This flexibility, as I see it, is due not so much to techniques radically different from the *Arcadia* poems but to his success at making familiar modes of discourse—speech rhythms, logical structures, imagery, and personification—modify each other variously and differently. We have seen the symmetrical balance of full-blown praise evoked for its own undoing; the strong, cumulative balance of such a figure as climax giving way to direct, informal speech; the logical patterns of cause and effect and contrast underlying the imagery of meditation; and the lively results of personification. In these Sidney's habit of arranging autonomous, redundant patterns of rhythm is checked or modified and made serviceable. In these also we may see the energy of Sidney's style as a medium for thoughtful poetry.

Although it is risky and sometimes false to make too near a connection between a poet's work and his stated preference in style—in Sidney's case a revealing, as opposed to an embellishing medium—

it is at least possible to regard the sequence and a few of the *Certaine Sonets* as an effort to satisfy this aim. As the *Defence* informs us, Sidney articulates his position in the rhetorical traditions of his time, and it would be futile to discuss his objectives and achievements while ignoring those traditions. But, like his contemporaries, he assumed that the devices of style were superadded to the subject, where modern criticism would prefer to see them as reflections of modes of thought, postulating for any and all style a more intimate unity between "manner and matter." No doubt any idea, if stated crudely and loosely enough, may bear a variety of expressions, but in a more precise sense a change in style necessitates a change in the idea. And the details of Sidney's expression, especially when they show us different styles in various mixtures, announce particular and local shadings given to ideas generally seen as conventional themes. The ample and traditional Platonic moralizing of Sonnet 71 is broken apart and transformed by the intrusion of wit in its last line: "But ah, Desire still cries, give me some food." In another poem, this time outside the sequence, a particular mingling of devices reports, within the broad limits of a conventional motif, a particular tone and shading of attitude:

> Thou blind mans marke, thou fooles selfe chosen snare,
> Fond fancies scum, and dregs of scattred thought,
> Band of all evils, cradle of causelesse care,
> Thou web of will, whose end is never wrought.

The proportioned fullness of these lines might very well place them within the compass of the *Arcadia* verse. There is a definition of the sexual appetite in the phrases, but it is their intensity that we notice. The obvious alliteration and nearly uniform placing of the caesura are characteristic of Sidney in his more ornamental moods. In the second quatrain Sidney continues to use repetition and he still alliterates, but he shifts his focus from the general to the particular:

> Desire, desire I have too dearely bought,
> With prise of mangled mind thy worthlesse ware,
> Too long, too long asleepe thou hast me brought,
> Who should my mind to higher things prepare.

And in the sestet the devices of repetition are set in a more clearly logical context:

> But yet in vaine thou hast my ruine sought,
> In vaine thou madest me to vaine things aspire,
> In vaine thou kindlest all thy smokie fire.
> For vertue hath this better lesson taught,
> Within my selfe to seeke my onelie hire:
> Desiring nought but how to kill desire.

In structure this sonnet is reminiscent of Sonnet 39, the apostrophe to sleep, and like it maintains an even surface tone closer to impersonal formality and deliberately planned thought than to the informality of surprise. Both poems fail to mirror the mind in agitated, uncertain conflict, but "Thou blind mans marke" is especially notable as a piece of meditation. It is one of the finest examples of the meditative neatness which Louis Martz singles out as Sidney's contribution to the lyric of his age,[15] and its failure to translate the sensibility through the casual immediacy of dramatic speech is compensated by other virtues. The imagery is wide ranging and, for Sidney, quite vivid. Sidney approaches Shakespeare's ability to make a sonnet powerful through metaphor, and the imagery is supported by the judiciously varied word repetition, which here prepares for and intensifies the word play of the final line. "Thou blind mans marke" offers us an image of sober and powerfully deliberate emotional intensity. It moves close to the patterned ornament of Spenserian verse but stops short of the point where ornament seems to become the whole interest of the style.

"Thou blind mans marke" is a final reminder that Sidney's most finished verse is never committed to one mode of expression, never fixed in a single adjustment of the elements of rhythm, rhetoric, and imagery. For as we move from poem to poem they appear in slightly different relations to one another. Sidney can write verse that is dramatic, dramatic and thoughtful, thoughtful and deliberate, argumentative or plaintive. A less plastic style would have reduced his love lyric to skilled experiment in conventional formula, but the sequence with its meditative strain and its frequent approaches to dialogue and direct speech confronts us not with the gymnastics of a polished stylist but with a mind examining and arguing about the conditions of its own being. For this task a flexible style (perhaps the reason why *Astrophel and Stella* has sometimes been called disconnected, a collec-

---

[15] *The Poetry of Meditation*, p. 266.

tion of love poems written at different times and loosely gathered together) is admirably suited. It allows Sidney to reflect the mind of the lover in as many moods and from as many angles as he wishes.

Perhaps the most frequent of these moods is introspection. The volume of poems taking the form of miniature debates is large, and although Astrophel's self-examination is a development of forces present in the love lyric at least as early as Petrarch, Sidney magnifies the importance of this strain, altering the traditional balance between the introspective and purely expressive in the Petrarchan convention. The "plainness" of his style, to the extent that it encourages dramatic analysis of the mind and feelings, looks forward to the "thinking verse" of Shakespeare, Donne, and Herbert, and allows a kind of poetry that Hallett Smith has described as analyzing the emotions it expresses.[16] It speaks persuasively to the poetic interests of our own generation.

[16] *Elizabethan Poetry*, p. 133.

7.

Astrophel and Stella: "Reasons Audíte"[1]

*O*ne's first impression of *Astrophel and Stella* is apt to be a sense of its bewildering variety in style and motif. Most of the first thirty sonnets appear derivative and have often been read as standard exercises in Petrarchan adoration, witty, conceited, and somewhat too ornate. They are followed by poems more somber in mood, other "Petrarchan" sonnets, some frank expressions of sexual desire, and pieces of restless self-analysis. Moreover, one easily recognizes poems dwelling on standard topics—the lover's restless nights, addresses to friends, appeals for "grace," remarks directed to a river, the moon, or a highway, expressions of the warfare in his heart, and complaints against Cupid. Tournaments, a dog, a sparrow, and the act of poetic composition serve as occasions for the display of Astrophel's feelings. Love seems to assume all guises, to be sacred and profane, witty, gay, sad, somber, angry, shrill, or exhausted. All occasions suit it, all incidents furnish images for its expression.

[1] This chapter appeared, in somewhat different form, as an article, "Reason, Passion, and Introspection in Sidney's *Astrophel and Stella," Texas Studies in English*, XXXVI (1957), 127–140.

In the face of such a poetic kaleidescope one is virtually forced to search out some guiding principle or structure within the work to justify its status as a "sequence," or rest content, as some critics have done, to regard it as near, but meaningful, anarchy.[2] For the latter view, the term "sequence" does not apply at all, and such local patterns as there are between sonnets are evidence either that the author experimented more than once with commonplaces or that some repetition was necessary to avoid total chaos. The danger in looking for a greater coherence in *Astrophel and Stella* is that we may look too hard and reduce its quite real variety to an oversimplification which can only partly define the character of the work. For example, it is tempting to see a plot behind the brief, though frequent, allusions to the circumstances of Astrophel's life; but a number of sonnets might conceivably be differently placed without any damage to such plot development as there is, and a record of outward events in a love affair is certainly not the center of interest in *Astrophel and Stella.* Or one might agree with Nashe whose description—"the argument cruell chastitie, the Prologue hope, the Epilogue dispaire"[3]—reads an emotional sequence into the poems. There are clusters of poems which develop one mood and another, but they do not succeed each other as steadily as Nashe implies. Rather, joy, melancholy, despair, wry self-accusation, complaint, praise, anger, bitterness, and ecstasy weave in and out through the entire range of the work, and a number of poems are mixed in mood and feeling. Furthermore, Sidney chose no obvious objective structure, unlike Spenser, who binds his *Amoretti* to the four seasons and through them traces the course of his emotions.

Nevertheless, *Astrophel and Stella* has an order, just as it has variety, and the first principle in that order has been ably demonstrated by Richard B. Young, whose reading of the sequence is the most successful and convincing yet to appear.[4] Young justifies the changing style of the work as prompted by the several and changing roles of the protagonist. In the early sonnets Astrophel assumes the guise of the traditional poet-lover, conventional in his praise of Stella and conven-

[2] The most eloquent exponent of this view is C. S. Lewis; see *English Literature in the Sixteenth Century Excluding Drama*, pp. 326 ff.

[3] From the preface to Thomas Newman's first 1591 quarto edition of *Astrophel and Stella*. The preface is available in *Elizabethan Critical Essays*, ed. G. Gregory Smith, II, 223 ff.

[4] *English Petrarke: A Study in Sidney's Astrophel and Stella*, pp. 40–88.

tional even in protesting the sincerity and uniqueness of his love. As his involvement with her deepens (e.g. Sonnet 37), his attitude becomes less posed, his response to her coldness more and more ironic, and the notes of his utterance more discordant and contrasted. Through the Eighth Song he alternates between complaint and moments of near-euphoria as he finds his affection gradually, but hesitantly, reciprocated and looks forward to the physical possession of Stella. When this fails, he returns at the end of the sequence to more conventional despair, retreating, as it were, behind the mask of literary tradition.

This account of the motives for Sidney's changing expression has much to recommend it. It does not depend upon proving the autobiographical truth of the sequence, it carefully links Sidney's work to the literary traditions he inherited, and it recognizes the central importance of a dramatically active sensibility in measuring the quality of the verse. Moreover, it relieves criticism of the false position of accepting those poems which appear to move farthest from traditional utterance and seem most directly expressive of "real" emotions, while rejecting the highly conceited and mythological sonnets as stiff exercises in imitation of familiar Petrarchan formulas. Rather, in Young's view both types are part of Sidney's total and deliberate artistic purpose.

But Young's interpretation needs further testing. He is correct to remind us that the later sonnets show Astrophel returning to the pose of the literary lover, reverting to the conventions he has apparently denied. Astrophel's reversion, provoked by his failure to persuade Stella to succumb, finds expression in the familiar "contraries" by which the frustrated but still adoring lover is commonly identified. Thus, according to Young's reading,

By the end of the sequence, through his relation to Stella, Astrophel has been made aware of the nature of Love as the Petrarchan universal: he has discovered himself as part of the convention, which, by virtue of his participation in it, has acquired permanent validity.[5]

In accepting the outcome of the sequence as a vindication of the Petrarchan code, these remarks imply that there is a resolution of the

[5] The same, p. 88.

102

tension between what is, broadly speaking, Astrophel's sensualism and his idealism, at least to the extent that he has learned to live with frustration and to accept Stella's value as an object of worship.

This interpretation raises some questions. The tone of the final sonnets is close to psychological paralysis, leaving Astrophel in a condition of moral and emotional ambiguity, and Young is quite correct in insisting that such a state is well within the convention. But it is proper to ask whether Astrophel's validation of the convention is one that approves its idealism or recognizes the painful reality of its contradictions. There is another problem, and it is one that has some bearing on the first. If we regard the main conflict of *Astrophel and Stella* as the standard opposition between the literary and realistic roles of the lover, that is, a tension between amorous idealism and plain sexuality, we overlook another set of standards, based on the dialectics of Renaissance psychology, which complicate the simple test of strength between idealism and sexual aggression. The hallowed conflict of reason and passion, based on the putative superiority of man's rational understanding over his animal lust, thoroughly informs *Astrophel and Stella,* and it is towards this conflict that Astrophel's introspection gravitates, leading him to question his idealism on rational grounds, as well as on the grounds of circumstance which Young has noticed. It is therefore impossible to see reason as a support for idealism, for it judges the impulse to worship just as it judges the passions.

The use of a standard of rationalism to gauge the passions is at least as old as Plato's *Phaedrus,* which is, paradoxically, one of the sources of the idealistic amorism in Western literature. Petrarchan verse occasionally broaches the conflict of reason and passion but seldom consistently or with the same force which Sidney, and after him Shakespeare and Fulke Greville, were able to exert. And in the work of the latter three, the ultimate effect of the struggle is to undercut the devotional basis of Petrarchan attitudes. Its terms are so familiar in classical and Renaissance literature that it has scarcely received more than passing notice in Sidney's work until the recent commentaries of Hallett Smith and J. W. Lever. Both men have urged the effectiveness of the conflict of reason and passion for dramatizing Astrophel's mental states. Lever remarks that "Sidney was more concerned with understanding himself than with edifying his readers," and that there-

103

fore "Reason, Virtue, and Sense were given parts in miniature allegorical episodes, not unlike the comic scenes of contemporary Interludes."[6] Smith sees the contest between reason and passion as "extended and pervasive" and underlines its convenience in organizing the protagonist's varied moods and motives:

The arguments of Virtue or Reason . . . can be catalogued and conceded, refuted, or twisted in a sophistic way so that they serve as a tribute to Stella. Rhetorically, this argument is more fruitful than any other for the purpose of the sonnets. The poet can treat the precepts of virtue with a tone of impatience, resignation, triumphant superiority; he can use them for his own position or against it.[7]

These views are close together and are essentially correct. But while they underscore the psychological reality of many of the poems, they present the dialectics of Astrophel's mental conflict mainly as an artistic tool handy to Sidney's purpose, the implication being that any other set of ideas might do as well. These concepts are in fact much more: they are intimately concerned in the process by which Astrophel sees his own experience and evaluates it, and they are responsible, I suspect, for the underlying seriousness with which the love affair is treated.

Although familiar in its broadest terms, the issue in question needs some review to make clear its bearing on the details of the sequence. It derives from a concept of the human soul as made up of rational and irrational (or passionate) principles, a concept shared by Plato and Aristotle and easily discovered in a host of later theorists. According to Aristotle these principles are in harmony only when the rational can govern the irrational:

For we praise the rational principle of the continent man and of the incontinent, and the part of their soul that has such a principle, since it urges them aright and toward the best objects; but there is found in them also another element naturally opposed to the rational principle, which fights against and resists that principle . . . or shares in it, in so far as it listens to it and obeys it.[8]

---

[6] *The Elizabethan Love Sonnet*, p. 84.

[7] *Elizabethan Poetry*, p. 154.

[8] *Nichomachean Ethics*, 1102^{b}15–30, in *The Basic Works of Aristotle*, ed. Richard McKeon (New York, 1941). For Aristotle's more complete account

To assume that the two principles are naturally hostile leads to the notion that reason is, or should be, the instrument of self-control when the passions are stirred. Yet reason alone cannot originate action; though "mind" may conceive the objects of action, some element of desire is always necessary.[9]

The Renaissance accepted these fundamentals both as an ethic and as a description of the realities of human psychology, and many authorities expounded them in detail. Here we need recognize only the general features:

In man, the rational soul is the ruling power, and the sensitive faculties are its servants. It has two divisions—intellectual and volitional that is, *reason* and *will*. The former . . . seeks truth through a logical train of thought. It draws conclusions regarding truth and falsehood, good and evil; in other words it is capable of judgment. The reason determines what is good and what is evil and informs the will of its conclusions.[10]

But the will may be corrupted by the passions, and the understanding may be obscured by them. "Sin, therefore, as the result of passion may arise through either cause, blindness of understanding, or perversion of the will."[11]

In a general context, Sidney evokes the antagonism of reason and passion in the *Arcadia* poem, "Since natures workes be good, and death doth serve" (*Works*, II, 166). Aside from the familiar pieces, "Thou blind mans marke, thou fooles self chosen snare" and "Leave me ô love, which reachest but to dust," two other poems in *Certaine Sonets* are similarly informed: "When Love puft up with rage of hy disdaine" and "If I could thinke how these my thoughts to leave."

---

of the soul, see *De Anima*, especially 413ª20–414ª25 and 427ᵇ5 ff. Plato's concept of the soul as split between rational and irrational principles informs most of his work. See *Phaedo*, 65–66 ff., *Philebus*, 31 ff., 61, and *Republic*, IV, 439, in *The Dialogues of Plato*, trans. Benjamin Jowett (New York, 1937), reprinted from the 3rd ed. (Oxford, 1892).

[9] *De Anima*, 432ᵇ20–433ª25.

[10] Lawrence W. Babb, *The Elizabethan Malady* (East Lansing, 1951), p. 4. Babb furnishes informative lists of authorities for these concepts. It is also worth noting that Sidney relies slightly on the physiology of love melancholy, which Babb (Chaps. 1, 2, and 6) describes in detail. See Sonnets 1, 16, 96, and 98.

[11] Lily B. Campbell, *Shakespeare's Tragic Heroes, Slaves of Passion* (Cambridge, 1930), p. 99.

105

The former describes the melancholy resulting from the "bondage" of reason to virtuous beauty; in the latter the poet recounts love's power to subdue reason to sense, his inability to "thinke what thoughts were best to thinke," and concludes:

> But since my thoughts in thinking still are spent,
>   With reasons strife, by senses overthrowne,
>   You fairer still, and still more cruell bent,
>   I loving still a love that loveth none.
>   I yeeld and strive, I kisse and curse the paine:
>   Thought, reason, sense, time, you, and I, maintaine.

This version of the improper workings of the soul (and its implied orderly function) directly inspires Astrophel's account of his struggles with his emotions, and the fact that Sidney has worked with the same dialectic outside the sequence merely reinforces belief in its necessary role in his concept of love.

In the early poems of the sequence the hostility of reason and passion, emerges as wilful argument against the counsels of virtue:

> *Vertue* alas, now let me take some rest,
>   Thou setst a bate betweene my will and wit,
>   If vaine love have my simple soule opprest:
>   Leave what thou likest not, deale not thou with it.

Yet virtue can still claim the weakened support of reason:

> But if that needs thou wilt usurping be,
>   The litle reason that is left in me,
>   And still th'effect of thy perswasions prove.
>   (Sonnet 4)

Sonnet 10 pursues the theme, with Astrophel still the Devil's advocate, admonishing reason because it ignores the promptings of "sense" and appetite:

> Reason, in faith thou art well serv'd, that still
>   Wouldst brabling be with sence and love in me:
>   I rather wisht thee clime the Muses hill,
>   Or reach the fruite of Natures choisest tree,

106

Or seeke heav'ns course, or heav'ns inside to see:
> Why shouldst thou toyle our thornie soile to till?
> Leave sense, and those which senses objects be:
> Deale thou with powers of thoughts, leave love to will.

But thou wouldst needs fight both with love and sence,
> With sword of wit, giving wounds of dispraise,
> Till downe-right blowes did foyle thy cunning fence.

The tone and verbal structure of these lines, their impatience and annoyance and treatment of reason as a bothersome meddler, plainly discover that the failure of reason as an instrument of moral control is consciously and deliberately willed by Astrophel. His very acknowledgment of traditional dialectical terms eliminates blindness of understanding as a cause of error.

Wilful error is for that reason not precisely a retreat into unreason. Rather Astrophel seeks to invert the normal efficacy of his moral judgment in the immediate crisis. Reason must no longer dictate to the sensitive appetite but should devote itself to impersonal matters: literature ("clime the Muses hill"), natural science ("reach the fruite of Natures choisest tree"), astronomy ("seeke heav'ns course"), and theology ("heav'ns inside to see"). Dealing with "powers of thoughts" suggests a purely contemplative role for the intellect, but the contemplative use of reason divorced from personal moral experience does not represent the goal of Astrophel's struggle, only a briefly considered alternative. Ultimately his mind gropes for the kind of understanding Sidney mentions in the *Defence*: "The highest end of the mistresse knowledge . . . stands . . . in the knowledge of a mans selfe, in the Ethike and Politique consideration, with the end of well doing, and not of well knowing onely."[12]

But the issues in the early poems show Astrophel of two minds. On the one hand, he attempts to dignify his passion for Stella on rational grounds, adopting the familiar posture of the Platonic lover by admitting that reason cannot banish desire, but may prove the worthiness of its object:

> Reason thou kneel'dst, and offeredst straight to prove,
> By reason good, good reason her to love.
>
> (Sonnet 10)

[12] *Works*, III, 11.

Stella becomes, for the time being, the personification of an almost religious adoration.[13] Yet from a Scholastic point of view, such a compromise is radical error. In the Thomistic doctrine of the process of sin the religious and moral dignity which Astrophel, aided by his reason, furnishes to love is sophistry. Platonic, courtly devotion, representing only one of the impulses to which he is subject, thus comes under the pressure of critical reason, and the poems exhibiting this critical temper begin, even in the early moments of the sequence, to contradict his more sanguine moods. Not one, but two, forms of reason act in *Astrophel and Stella*: the first yields to love after a token struggle, but the second resists and disapproves.

In Sonnet 5 Astrophel reviews the possible dangers of wilful illusion, though finally deciding that he cannot and does not wish to escape them:

> It is most true, that eyes are form'd to serve
> > The inward light: and that the heavenly part
> > Ought to be king, from whose rules who do swerve,
> > Rebels to Nature strive for their owne smart.
>
> It is most true, what we call *Cupids* dart,
> > An image is, which for our selves we carve;
> > And, fooles, adore in temple of our hart,
> > Till that good God make Church & Churchman starve.
>
> True, that true Beautie Vertue is indeed,
> > Whereof this Beautie can be but a shade,
> > Which elements with mortall mixture breed:
>
> True, that on earth we are but pilgrims made,
> > And should in soule up to our countrey move:
> > True, and yet true that I must *Stella* love.

The extended recognition of what constitutes a proper balance in the soul (with reason pre-eminent) explores the ways in which this balance may suffer (by a self-willed exchange of love for religious devotion), ponders the distinctness of divine and mortal beauty (Stella is merely an imperfect copy of "true" beauty), and, finally, acknowledges the

[13] See Plato, *Phaedrus*, 251–252, and Castiglione in *Three Renaissance Classics*, ed. Burton A. Milligan, p. 608.

108

Platonic and Christian vision of man's life as a pilgrimage from the unreality of this life to the reality of heaven. But the Platonic sanction involved here should be distinguished from the sublimated eroticism derived from the *Phaedrus*. Apparently Sidney invokes one feature of Platonism to contradict another, for here in Sonnet 5 Astrophel for a moment denies the validity of sensory experience and dwells on its discontinuity with spiritual truth.[14] Cupid is only a projection of inner desire, and flesh is merely flesh.

Furthermore, line fourteen cannot stand simply as a flat denial of this structure of orthodox belief; it suggests as well a running conflict in Astrophel's mind between religious and erotic impulses, between spiritual and amorous conventions. (Even within the Petrarchan convention the poem draws on conventionally antagonistic attitudes: a similar division informs Petrarch's sequence over its entire range, though Sidney's treatment generally differs tonally. It might be said that the nexus of conventions in Sonnet 5 is both Petrarchan and anti-Petrarchan, though anti-Petrarchism is usually a matter of denying the silliness of an exaggerated literary pose.[15]) The fact that Astrophel's conflict is internal and occurs prior to any action on his part helps us to specify its debt to Scholastic doctrine. Unworthy behavior does not determine his error; his preference for Stella as worthy of devotion does. For "mortal sin," according to Aquinas, "consists in turning away from our last end, which is God, which turning away pertains to the deliberating reason, whose function it is also to direct towards the end."[16] The intellectuality of Astrophel's sin is matched by the intellectuality of his early feelings for Stella. It may be argued that beneath the moral issues and the appeal of Stella's virtue and beauty lies an essentially physical urge, but his sense of what is hap-

[14] Platonic dualism appears explicitly in *Phaedo*, 65–66.

[15] See Robert J. Clements, *Critical Theory and Practice of the Plèiade*, pp. 23–31.

[16] *The "Summa Theologica" of Saint Thomas Aquinas*, trans. Fathers of The English Dominican Province, rev. ed., 3 vols. (New York, 1947), I–II, 77.8. I am indebted for my outline of the Scholastic background to James V. Cunningham, "Tragic Effect and Tragic Process in Some Plays of Shakespeare and Their Background in the Literary and Ethical Theory of Classical Antiquity and the Middle Ages" (Stanford University diss., 1945); see especially p. 302. Cunningham is the first to notice the importance of Scholastic doctrine for *Astrophel and Stella*, but this portion of his dissertation has not, so far as I know, been published.

pening to him and the tone of the verse is only remotely carnal. Frankly avowed sexuality emerges only in later poems and there opposes the more Platonic, "pure" emotion. In the introductory Sonnet 2, on the other hand, it is "knowne worth" that first saps his resistance, and in the same poem he remarks, "I saw and liked," a phrase reminiscent of the process which Aquinas defines as "concupiscence of the eyes" and regards as mental, not "fleshly."[17] When appetite triumphs over the counsels of reason, the initial result is not overt adultery but misplaced idealistic devotion.

None the less, one might expect that the easy victory of passion, so explicitly acted out in Sonnets 4, 5, and 10 (the drama is repeated in Sonnet 14), should mean that reason would no longer make a difference. If this were true, the melancholy conclusion of the sequence would stem only from Astrophel's frustrated suit. Frustration is, of course, a prominent motif—it helps organize the narrative movement —but it fails to account for those meditative and introspective verses in which the reasoning faculty becomes an agent of self-discovery and evaluation. When Astrophel pauses to reflect, the struggle between reason and passion revives, and his state of mind, as well as the status of his affair with Stella, becomes crucial to the total development of the sequence. As a result he may, at any given moment, understand what has happened to him but lack the will to subdue his appetite. In the same breath he tries to analyze and rationalize his emotions, and this simultaneity of wayward volition and rational understanding epitomizes the quality of the entire work. It is so presented in Sonnet 2:

> Now even that footstep of lost libertie
>   Is gone, and now like slave-borne *Muscovite*,
>   I call it praise to suffer Tyrannie;
>
> And now employ the remnant of my wit,
>   To make me selfe beleeve, that all is well,
>   While with a feeling skill I paint my hell.

Dismay at Stella's coldness is thus insufficient to explain Astrophel's distress, nor can Sidney's account of the clash between religious and erotic impulses be safely dismissed as standard emotional hyperbole

---

[17] *Summa Theologica*, I–II, 77.5.

or the mere dignifying of witty exercises in composition. In spite of its verbal play, Sonnet 18, one of the most searching of the early poems, is thoroughly serious and unmistakably central.

> With what sharpe checkes I in my selfe am shent,
>> When into Reasons audite I do go:
>> And by just counts my selfe a banckrout know
>> Of all those goods, which heav'n to me have lent:
>
> Unable quite to pay even Natures rent,
>> Which unto it by birthright I do ow:
>> And which is worse, no good excuse can show,
>> But that my wealth I have most idly spent.
>
> My youth doth waste, my knowledge brings forth toyes,
>> My wit doth strive those passions to defend,
>> Which for reward spoile it with vaine annoyes.
>
> I see my course to loose my selfe doth bend:
>> I see and yet no greater sorow take
>> Then that I loose no more for *Stellas* sake.

Previously discussed for its logical strategy, Sonnet 18 can now be seen in the dialectical pattern of Astrophel's introspective drive. There is, in other words, a convergence of "manner and matter" such as Sidney contemplated in the *Defence*. And this indictment of love and its consequences, reached through the systematic disposition of trope, has its origins in standards identical to those in Sonnet 5: ultimately Astrophel owes his endowments and his allegiance to heaven, and this debt measures the seriousness of his prodigality. Yet once again his weighing of the moral issues confronts him with the mysterious psychological condition in which understanding is helpless to control the will or passions, a discontinuity immediately rephrased in Sonnet 19:

> On *Cupids* bow how are my heart-strings bent
>> That see my wracke, and yet embrace the same?

There is no failure of emotional intensity in these lines, but their remarkable quality is their degree of self-consciousness. And the direction of the early stages of the sequence can be traced through the awareness of the internal struggles it discovers and encompasses. This movement is by no means steady or uninterrupted: Sonnets 21 and 28, for instance, reveal Astrophel sensitive to "shame" but also mark brief reversions to an unreflective confidence lacking in Sonnets 18 and 19. Stella's coyness (Sonnets 31 and 32) provides the occasion for somber melancholy of another sort, and other poems explore his attempts to write (Sonnets 1, 3, 6, and 15) or praise her and reiterate his devotion in various ways (Sonnets 7–9, 11–13, 16, 17, 20, 22, 23, 25–27, and 29). Incidentally, Richard B. Young's reading of *Astrophel and Stella* suggests convincingly that this latter group does not so much represent Sidney's indulgence in conventional and mediocre artistry as it is expressive of Astrophel's conventionalized feelings.[18] What the more introspective poems achieve is to punctuate these with doubt and uncertainty.

An added motive for Astrophel's skeptical melancholy emerges in later poems. The controversial Sonnet 33 appears to be a momentary repudiation of moral controversy, for Astrophel, discovering Stella to be the property of another, now regrets that his preoccupation with intellectual subleties has kept his relations with her discreet. But as Sonnet 34 (a debate between his "wit" and self) demonstrates, the need to turn inward remains undiminished, and pondering the difficulty of writing under emotional and moral pressure, he concludes:

> What idler thing, then speake and not be hard?
> What harder thing then smart, and not to speake?
> Peace foolish wit, with wit my wit is mard.
>
> Thus write I while I doubt to write, and wreake
> My harmes on Inks poore losse, perhaps some find
> *Stellas* great powrs, that so confuse my mind.

And his concern for his own mental state remains uppermost in Sonnet 40, for Stella has managed to reach his pride:

---

[18] The poem is usually interpreted as Sidney's discovery that Penelope Devereux had married Lord Rich, though Grosart, *The Complete Poems of Sir Philip Sidney*, 3 vols., I, lvii, argues that it merely reflects his disappointment at having missed a rendezvous with her. The bitterness and self-reproach in it would seem to grow from something more crucial. It is at least plain that Astrophel for the moment feels alienated from Stella ("I find how heav'nly day wretch I did misse"; "Hart rent thy selfe . . . no force, no fraud, robd thee of thy delight") and feels that hesitation has lost him his chance.

> O *Stella* deare, how much thy power hath wrought,
> That hast my mind, none of the basest, brought
> My still kept course, while other[s] sleepe to mone.

Similar utterances are spaced through the more completely expressive verse of the middle of the sequence, and there is an increasing economy of reference to the details of mental turbulence. Sonnets 41 and 43 mark one more attempt to accept the Platonic pose and forego open sexual desire, but Sonnet 44 prefaces a complaint of Stella's lack of pity with the declaration that his "mind bemones his sense of inward smart." And Sonnet 47 is an urgent reassessment of the cost of his devotion:

> What have I thus betrayed my libertie?
>   Can those blacke beames such burning markes engrave
>   In my free side? or am I borne a slave,
>   Whose necke becomes such yoke of tyranny?
>
> Or want I sense to feele my miserie?
>   Or sprite, disdaine of such disdaine to have?
>   Who for long faith, tho dayly helpe I crave,
>   May get no almes but scorne of beggerie.
>
> Vertue awake, Beautie but beautie is,
>   I may, I must, I can, I will, I do
>   Leave following that, which it is gaine to misse.
>
> Let her go: soft, but here she comes, go to,
>   Unkind, I love you not: O me, that eye
>   Doth make my heart give to my tongue the lie.

"That which it is gaine to misse" effectively recalls the religiously informed skepticism of the earlier poems, while the shame and self-reproach of the octave are sufficient testimony of Astrophel's wounded self-esteem, and the need for "almes" seems more than a demand for recognition. The motive of physical possession is implicit and insistent, and although the idealistic tributes to Stella's beauty and virtue reveal him still inclined to Platonic devotion, it is equivocated by the increasingly aggressive demands of his libido. Finally, we may recall that here in Sonnet 47 Sidney's flexible style serves to translate this complex of warring impulses from a meditative to a dramatically immediate mode of presentation. Astrophel's comparatively detached perspicuity becomes involved in the crisis of the active will ("Let her go") and retreats at the sign of superior force ("That eye"). Several poems later he acknowledges the difficulty and frustration of his attempt at mental clarity and control:

> Now I wit-beaten long by hardest Fate,
> So dull am, that I cannot looke into
> The ground of this fierce *Love* and lovely hate.
>
> (Sonnet 60)

Yet even the impassioned Sonnet 64, a direct appeal for Stella's surrender, shows him still answering to the moral standards he violates and the shame he risks:

> No more, my deare, no more these counsels trie,
> O give my passions leave to run their race:
> Let Fortune lay on me her worst disgrace,
> Let folke orecharg'd with braine against me crie.
>
> Let clouds bedimme my face, breake in mine eye,
> Let me no steps but of lost labour trace:
> Let all the earth with scorne recount my case,
> But do not will me from my *Love* to flie.

Here the psychology is more complex than one might suppose: line eight may be simply a plea to be allowed to remain in Stella's presence, but the capitalization and italicization of "*Love*" suggest a reference to Cupid and therefore to Astrophel's own emotion. The ambiguity may quite reasonably be interpreted to include a compulsive wish to cling to passion as well as the more obvious desire to remain at Stella's side. Read in these terms the line announces Astrophel's commitment both to his mistress and to the wilful nourishing of something within, despite all consequence.

On the surface, then, Astrophel's discontent is born of the clash between Stella's reticence and his desire for reciprocal passion and surrender, but this outward conflict is steadily deepened and particularized:

114

And do I see some cause a hope to feede,
    Or doth the tedious burd'n of long wo
    In weakened minds, quicke apprehending breed,
    Of everie image, which may comfort show?

I cannot brag of word, much lesse of deed,
    Fortune wheeles still with me in one sort slow,
    My wealth no more, and no whit lesse my need,
    Desire still on the stilts of feare doth go.
              (Sonnet 66)

However, in the sestet Astrophel announces that Stella may relent and grant him her "favor," at first simply a concession to his idealistic devotion. She has urged him to accept a "chast" love in Sonnets 61 and 62; but in Sonnets 66 and 67 she seems more receptive. In these circumstances Astrophel's need to look within himself is less urgent, and he adopts the role of the persistent seducer. There follows a series of largely emotive poems (including the Fifth through the Ninth Songs); for the most part these are empty of serious moral questioning or internal discord, qualities that return only when the lovers separate in Sonnet 87.[19]

In the latter Astrophel no longer doubts Stella's affection for him; rather he hovers between sadness that she weeps at their parting and joy that she feels strongly enough to be so moved. Yet the conclusion reaches beyond and behind a simple expression of these mixed feelings:

Thus, while the 'ffect most bitter was to me,
    And nothing then the cause more sweet could be,
    I had bene vext, if vext I had not beene.

This capacity to understand the satisfaction of the ego in the midst of sympathetic melancholy is enhanced by the narrative structure: the separation has already occurred, and Astrophel looks back at it to meditate the ambivalence of his response and its causes. Sidney's method gauges the intensity of emotion only on the surface; its main achievement is to allow the speaker to analyze his own state of mind,

---

[19] Except 68, 71, and 72, which are sophistical rationalizations of sexual desire.

to discover the sources of feeling. And Astrophel's discovery prompts the inference that he has become skeptical of the wholeness of his motives.

Sonnet 87 epitomizes one introspective procedure, but the relative placement of expressed feeling and its analysis is not always the same. Sonnet 88, by contrast, begins skeptically ("Out traytour absence, darest thou counsell me, / From my deare Captainnesse to run away?") but ends in a renewal of devotion. Yet the habit of painful meditation continually returns, and in Sonnet 94 Astrophel confesses his need for it as a vantage point of inner stability which he fears to lose:

> Griefe find the words, for thou hast made my braine
>> So darke with misty vapors, which arise
>> From out thy heavy mould, that inbent eyes
>> Can scarce discerne the shape of mine owne paine.[20]
>
> Do thou then (for thou canst) do thou complaine,
>> For my poore soule, which now that sicknesse tries,
>> Which even to sence, sence of it selfe denies,
>> Though harbengers of death lodge there his traine.

Here, as elsewhere, the effect of blending self-analysis with the context of expressed emotion is to deny the validity of idealism, to acknowledge the unsettling presence of physical desire, and to move attention away from Stella, her beauty, and her virtue.

At the same time, these meditations serve to rediscover the incurable commitment of the will, a perception at the heart of much Renaissance love poetry. As Shakespeare says, "My love is as a fever longing still / For that which nurseth the disease," and Sidney's version is so central to the entire range of *Astrophel and Stella* as to be the focal point of its conclusion. Sonnets 107 and 108 make an end to the sick melancholy begun in Sonnet 87, announcing a return of Astrophel's clarity of mind which had threatened to dissolve into incoherent grief (a "mazefull solitarinesse," as he calls it in Sonnet 96). The first, Sonnet 107 (lines 5–8), suggests a remedy for his compulsive attachment:

[20] Astrophel's disrupted thinking reflects symptoms of the late stages of love melancholy listed by Babb, *The Elizabethan Malady*, pp. 134–135, but the textbook lover is less introspective.

Sweete for a while give respite to my hart,
　　Which pants as though it stil should leape to thee:
　　And on my thoughts give thy Lieftenancy
　　To this great cause, which needes both use and art.[21]

And as a Queene, who from her presence sends
　　Whom she imployes, dismisse from thee my wit,
　　Till it have wrought what thy owne will attends.

But Sonnet 108 admits that no respite is at hand. Astrophel's sorrow is relieved by the joy that shines down from Stella, and yet his delight is simultaneously vitiated by sexual frustration and melancholy. He finally restates the condition in conventional paradox:

So strangely (alas) thy works in me prevaile,
　　That in my woes for thee thou art my joy,
　　And in my joyes for thee my only annoy.

Astrophel is thus forced to end as the standard Petrarchan lover, trapped by his own adoration but unable to hope for its satisfactions. The lines above must be read not as an announcement of the "validity" of that convention but as an admission of its hold on a mind unable to recover its independence and order. The resolution of the sequence lies in the irresolution of Astrophel.

It is possible that Sidney intended not to leave his work at this point: printed separately the two sonnets, "Thou blind mans Marke, thou fooles self chosen snare" and "Leave me ô Love, which reachest but to dust," provide an emphatic and disparaging analysis of the same mental and physical impulses to which Astrophel is subject, and they are often read, because of their repudiation of earthly in favor of heavenly

21 Lines seven and eight have usually been read as indicating some project Sidney was about to undertake. Pollard, *Sir Philip Sidney's Astrophel and Stella*, p. 226, thinks the allusion is to "Sidney's constant endeavors to obtain employment against Spain either in Holland or on the seas." Mona Wilson, *Astrophel & Stella*, p. 183, gives a most implausible interpretation: "I have no doubt that *Lieftenancy* alludes to the arrangement under discussion in the spring of 1582 by which Sir Henry was to return to Ireland as Lord Lieutenant, with Philip as his alleged successor." Such speculations read the lines too literally: Astrophel's "great cause" is the attempt to rid himself of his compulsive mental preoccupation with love and Stella, and he calls upon her for aid.

117

love, as terminating *Astrophel and Stella*.[22] Certainly if they did belong with it, Sidney would be even closer to Petrarch than he is, but similarity of subject is not evidence sufficient to ensure their place in the sequence. Moreover, in spite of Astrophel's frequent resort to orthodox religious and moral standards to test or criticize the quality of his emotions, there is no real preparation for a religious apotheosis. The attitude of Sonnet 108 is too firm to warrant such a sudden shift as the other two poems would represent. They would violate the dramatic tempo of the sequence as it stands and raise more questions of structure than they could possibly settle.

To admit, then, that *Astrophel and Stella* finishes more or less conventionally with its central figure juggling a paradox seems the best decision, but we must still recognize that Sidney has modified the convention to suit himself. For one thing, he has extended and deepened its tendency to introspection so that his work moves close to a total immersion in the ego of the hero. Where the literary and moral values of idealistic and idealized love dominate the rhapsodies and laments of most of Sidney's European predecessors, his own effort calls in another set of values to challenge the tradition. Where sexual desire is seldom more than a discreet hint in Petrarch, Desportes, Ronsard (I am thinking only of the sonnets), or Spenser, in Sidney it is frankly avowed and dramatically and psychologically indispensable. Astrophel accepts an unconsummated affair only because he has no other choice, not because he champions the value of idealistic devotion. Sidney, therefore, moves only within the broad perimeters of the Petrarchan convention. As C. S. Lewis says, he has written an "anatomy of love,"[23] or, more properly, he has dramatized the anatomy of the lover's mind.

At the same time Lewis's remark is meant to suggest a casual, even haphazard, order for *Astrophel and Stella*, not a deliberate and developed plan. But although the structure, or more properly the structures, of the sequence are discreetly managed and unobtrusive, they are nonetheless there. In this context, it is worthwhile to remember Nashe's description of the work: "The argument cruell chastitie, the

---

[22] Karl M. Murphy, "The 109th and 110th Sonnets of *Astrophel and Stella*," *PQ*, XXXIV (1955), 349–352, argues persuasively against their association with the sequence.

[23] *English Literature in the Sixteenth Century Excluding Drama*, p. 329.

Prologue hope, the Epilogue dispaire." [24] Nashe seizes upon the broadest movement of the sequence, Young examines the successive and related roles of Astrophel as lover, and I have pointed to the introspective pattern and its semidramatic unfolding. These structures are complementary, not exclusive, a fact which hints at the depth of Sidney's execution of his work and underscores once more the fundamental difference between *Astrophel and Stella* and the *Arcadia* verse.

Sidney was careful in both versions of the *Arcadia* to adjust the poems to the demands of the novel. In no important sense does the poetry carry the narrative structure,[25] but the individual lyrics lend to incidents a heightened emotional coloring. Even so the poems are isolable for study as distinct artistic performances. Technically, Sidney appears to have been interested in fashioning single poems, working out for each of them a tight and prominent internal order, generally moving, as we have noted, towards verbal and rhythmical symmetry. Yet the poems at the end of each book of the *Arcadia* reveal something else, a tendency to work with groups of poems related thematically or otherwise. These groups tend to be lightly connected by prose narrative links, but they are predominantly ceremonial in tone. The eclogues at the end of Book I in the old *Arcadia* have a mild dramatic interest, but Sidney's label, "Pastorall pastymes" (*Works*, IV, 87), is essentially accurate.

Astrophel and Stella, as an artistic whole, clearly moves further, both in concealing the structure which makes it a whole and in establishing, for English poetry at least, a broad, dramatically oriented context in which lyric develops the order and technique of larger forms. We can see the impact of such a development in the sonnet sequences of other and later poets (although most of them borrowed conceit and cliché without grasping the fictional principles Sidney used) and, more especially, in such a work as Herbert's *Temple*, which suggests a narrative substructure rather than making it explicit, and which renders the workings of mind and spirit without yielding to the chaos of separate lyrics brought together only through a general likeness of subject matter.

[24] G. Gregory Smith, *Elizabethan Critical Essays*, II, 223.

[25] It is not, however, simply fastened onto the prose text. For example, study the purpose of the short poems, "You living powers enclosed in stately shrine," and "My words, in hope to blaze my stedfast minde," (*Works*, I, 172–173), in their context.

To look back over the range of Sidney's poetry, then, is to find technical variety but not technical unevenness, and if we cannot establish a precise chronological development in artistic skill, we can do what is more satisfying—consider a poet whose work fulfilled its own internal principles and helped point many of the directions the English lyric was to take in the future.

APPENDICES

Appendix A

Definitions of Rhetorical Figures

*T*hese definitions are listed simply as a convenient reference for the reader and are placed here to avoid burdening the text with technical explanations. Needless to say, Sidney's use of formal rhetoric extends well beyond the few items listed here. I have discussed those which are most characteristic of his practice and which illustrate most clearly the various impulses and directions of his style. In the wording of the definitions I follow Veré Rubel, *Poetic Diction in the English Renaissance,* "Glossary of Rhetorical Figures," pp. 276–291. Miss Rubel, in turn, bases her definitions on those of Puttenham.

anadiplosis: repeating the last word or phrase of a line at the beginning of the next line.

anaphora: consecutive verses beginning with the same word or words. (This is probably the simplest and commonest of the figures of word repetition in English Renaissance verse.)

anthypophora: asking questions and answering them, either for argumentation, or for amplification, to emphasize a point.

antimetabole: repeating words in inverted order to contrast the meaning, often with the effect of wordplay.

antistrophe: repetition of the last word or phrase of a verse in succeeding verses—strictly speaking in successive verses. Miss Rubel lists six variant forms: 1) repeating the word or phrase at the end of the verse; 2) using identical words within a stanza; 3) repeating a word in the middle of successive lines; 4) repeating a word in the middle of stanzas that are near but not successive; 5) *antistrophe* through *antanaclasis* (homo-

123

nyms); 6) *antistrophe* through *traductio*. See below. (Sidney's most extensive use of the figure is in Sonnet 89, an example of the second variant, with "night" and "day" alternating as the rime words throughout the poem.)

asyndeton: a series of phrases, short clauses, or short sentences in parallel construction and without conjunctions. (Ordinarily Sidney uses *asyndeton* for the rapid, compressed listing of attributes, as in "Thou blind mans marke, thou fooles selfe chosen snare.")

climax: interlocking of words through a series of parallel constructions to show progression in the sense. (Puttenham's phrase, "the marching figure," aptly describes its effect.)

collectour: a form of *synathroesmus* used to close a passage or a poem; words, phrases, or short clauses which, by repetition, bind together what has been more fully treated before.

epanados: expansion of a statement by repeating each part with amplification. Similar to *prolepsis,* but the difference is that in *prolepsis* the key words of the original statement are not repeated in the amplification.

epizeuxis: repetition of a word or several words with no words intervening.

hirmus: a series of long phrases or subordinate clauses in parallel construction which precedes the main clause and hence gives an effect of periodicity.

merismus: presentation of a complete idea piecemeal. The difference between this figure and *synathroesmus* is that the purpose of *merismus* is analysis into parts of an idea which might otherwise be expressed in a single statement, whereas the purpose of *synathroesmus* is to gather into one heaping statement ideas which seem divergent.

ploce: repetition of a word, but with words intervening. (This figure occurs everywhere in Sidney's verse.)

prolepsis: making a general statement and then amplifying it.

prosonomasia: words similar in sound but not quite homonyms—used to give the effect of wordplay.

syllepsis: use of one word to supply several clauses, often with a punning effect.

synathroesmus: combining in one sentence parallel phrases or short clauses of different matter but all relating to a single idea.

traductio: repeating a word in different forms—a kind of wordplay.

124

Appendix B

The Blazon

The blazon appears in the following poems:

Arcadia: "What length of verse can serve brave *Mopsas* good to show?"
(I, 21).

"What toong can her perfections tell" (I, 218).

"O Words which fall like sommer deaw on me" (II, 18).

"Reason, tell me thy mind, if here be reason" (II, 236).

Astrophel and Stella:

Sonnets 9, 12, 77; First and Second Songs.

Certaine Sonets:

"Wo, wo, to me, on me return the smart."

Appendix C

Personification

Personification appears in the following poems:

Arcadia: "Come shepheards weedes, become your masters minde" (I, 113).

"In vaine, mine Eyes, you labour to amende" (I, 147).

"Let not old age disgrace my high desire" (I, 149).

"You living powres enclosed in stately shrine" (I, 172).

"My words, in hope to blaze my stedfast minde" (I, 173).

"Alas how long this pilgrimage doth last" (I, 227).

"Loved I am, and yet complaine of Love" (I, 253).

"Wyth two strange fires of equall heate possest" (I, 310).

"Thou Rebell vile, come, to thy master yelde" (I, 339).

"Faire rocks, goodly rivers, sweet woods, when shall I see peace?"
(I, 352).

"The Fire to see my woes for anger burneth" (I, 442).

"Since that to death is gone the shepheard hie" (I, 498).

"*Phaebus* farewell, a sweeter Saint I serve" (II, 5).

"Howe is my Sunn, whose beames are shining bright" (II, 9).

"O Words which fall like sommer deaw on me" (II, 18).

"Do not disdaine, ô streight up raised Pine" (II, 24).

"Sweete roote say thou, the roote of my desire" (II, 25).
"You goodly pines, which still with brave assent" (II, 25).
"Locke up, faire liddes, the treasure of my harte" (II, 26).
"Why doost thou haste away" (II, 32).
"O Stealing time the subject of delaie" (II, 32).
"My Lute which in thy selfe thy tunes enclose" (II, 35).
"When two Sunnes do appeare" (II, 38).
"*Aurora* now thou shewst thy blushing light" (II, 39).
"Get hence foule Griefe, the canker of the minde" (II, 50).
"Vertue, beawtie, and speach, did strike, wound, charme"
(II, 53).
"Let mother earth now decke her selfe in flowers" (II, 63).
"The ladd *Philisides*" (II, 70).
"Since wayling is a bud of causefull sorowe" (II, 138).
"Since that to death is gone the shepheard hie" (II, 139).
"Farewell ô Sunn, *Arcadias* clearest light" (II, 143).
"Fortune, Nature, Love, long have contended about me"
(II, 208).
"A Shepheards tale no height of stile desires" (II, 214).
"Reason, tell me thy mind, if here be reason" (II, 236).
"O sweet woods the delight of solitarines" (II, 237).
"Feede one my sheepe my chardge my comforte feede" (II, 238).
"Leave offe my sheepe yt is noe tyme to feede" (II, 238).
"Swete glove the swetenes of my secrett blisse" (II, 239).

Certaine Sonets:
"Since shunning paine, I ease can never find."
"When Love puft with rage of hy disdaine."
"The fire to see my wrongs for anger burneth."
"The Nightingale as soone as Aprill bringeth."
"The scourge of life, and deaths extreame disgrace."
"Wo, wo, to me, on me returne the smart."
"Thou paine the onely guest of loath'd constraint."
"And have I heard her say? ô cruell paine!"
"Like as the Dove which seeled up doth flie."
"My mistresse lowers and saith I do not love."
"In wonted walkes, since wonted fancies change."
"If I could thinke how these my thoughts to leave."
"What changes here, ô haire."
"Ring out your belles, let mourning shewes be spread."
"Thou blind mans marke, thou fooles selfe chosen snare."
"Leave me ô Love, which reachest but to dust."

126

Index

$\mathcal{A}$ll of Sidney's poems which are quoted, mentioned, or referred to are identified by their first lines, and the following designations are used for the works in which they appear: *A&S* with number *(Astrophel and Stella); CS (Certaine Sonets); LM (The Lady of May)*; Psalm with number *(The Psalms of David)*. No designation is used for the *Arcadia* poems. Poems listed in the appendices are not indexed unless they appear in the main body of the text.

Academie de poesie et de musique: 13 and n

"Ah bed, the field where joyes peace some do see . . ." *(A&S* 98): 105 n

"Alas, have I not paine enough my friend . . ." *(A&S* 14): 57, 93 n, 94, 110

"Alas, whence came this change of lookes? . . ." *(A&S* 86): 93 n

allegory: 34, 50–51, 54, 73, 104, 112. *See also* dream vision

alliteration: 12, 19, 29, 73, 97

anadiplosis: 33 n

anaphora: 12, 29, 44

"And do I see some cause a hope to feede . . ." *(A&S* 66): 85–86, 115

anthypophora: 81 n

anti-Ciceronianism: 65, 66–68. *See also* Cicero

anti-Petrarchism: 50, 51 n, 68, 109. *See also* Petrarchism

antithesis: 12, 18, 80, 93

Apollo (Phoebus): 41, 55, 91, 108, 112

Aquinas, Thomas: 109–110. *See also* Scholasticism

Arcadian Rhetorike, The: 66

Arcadia poems: 2, 6, 7, 9, 10, 11, 12, 20, 23, 24, 25, 30, 36, 38, 39, 40, 43, 44, 47, 48, 49, 52, 54, 55, 56, 58, 59, 62, 64, 70, 72, 73, 74, 75, 77, 78, 79, 81, 82, 83, 85, 86, 87, 89, 90, 96, 97, 119

Aristotle: 34, 104–105 and n

Arte of English Poesie, The: 4, 31

Arte of Reason, rightly termed, Witcraft, The: 66

Ascham, Roger: 13, 65

"As good to write as for to lie and grone . . ." *(A&S* 40): 112–113

"As I my little flocke on Ister banke . . .": 75

assonance: 12, 19, 29

Astrophel: 7, 39, 40, 55, 56, 57, 58, 62, 70, 72, 75, 78, 81, 83, 84, 85, 86, 89, 90, 91, 92, 93, 94, 95, 96, 99, 100, 101, 102, 103, 104, 106–119

Astrophel and Stella: 2–3, 7, 9, 10, 22, 25, 26, 29, 37, 39, 40, 43, 49, 51 n, 55, 56, 58, 62, 64, 69, 70, 72–74, 75, 76, 77, 78, 79, 80, 83, 85, 86, 89, 94, 97, 98, 100, 101, 102, 103, 108, 109 n, 112, 116, 118, 119

asyndeton: 31

Bacon, Francis: 5, 68

Baïf, Jean-Antoine de: 13 and n

Basilius: 55, 56

127

"Because I breathe not love to everie one . . ." (*A&S* 54): 93 n

"Because I oft in darke abstracted guise . . ." (*A&S* 27): 112

"Be your words made (good sir) of Indian ware . . ." (*A&S* 92): 80, 93 n

blazon: 36–37, 59

Book of the Courtier, The: 50, 52, 108 n

Campion, Thomas: 13, 14, 15 n

canzone: 50 and n

Castiglione, Baldassare: 50, 52, 108 n

Cavalcanti, Guido: 50

Certaine Sonets: 2, 9, 24, 25, 27, 57, 59, 62, 64, 74, 77, 97, 105

Cicero: 4, 30 and n, 31 and n, 65, 66, 68–69, 71, 72. *See also* anti-Ciceronianism

Ciceronianus (Erasmus): 65, 72

Ciceronianus (Harvey): 67–68

classical meter. *See* quantitative meter

climax: 84, 96

collectour, the: 31–32, 33

"Come *Dorus,* come . . .": 52, 55–56

"Come let me write . . ." (*A&S* 34): 69 n, 80–81, 85, 86, 112

"Come sleepe, ô sleepe . . ." (*A&S* 39): 98

conceit: 45, 54, 56 n, 60, 69, 73, 90, 91, 95

"Contre les Petrarquistes": 51 n

Convito: 50

Countesse of Pembroke's Arcadia, The (new *Arcadia*): 37, 52, 53, 55, 60, 62, 119

courtly love: 49, 50 n, 52–53. *See also* love; Petrarchism; Platonism

Cupid: 53, 95, 100, 108, 109, 111, 114

"*Cupid,* because thou shin'st in *Stellas* eyes . . ." (*A&S* 12): 91, 112

"curious wits seeing dull pensivenesse . . . , The" (*A&S* 23): 112

Daniel, Samuel: 51

Dante Alighieri: 50, 54

Davies, Sir John: 75

De Anima: 105 and n

Defence of Poesie, The: 15 n, 34 and n, 48, 64, 68–72, 82–83, 86, 97, 107, 111

Demosthenes: 66, 71. *See also* Wilson, Thomas

"Desire, though thou my old companion art . . ." (*A&S* 72): 93, 115 n

Desportes, Philippe: 51, 118

Devereux, Penelope (Lady Rich): 112 n

Diana: 59–60

Dicus: 14

dolce stil nuovo: 49

Donne, John: 6 n, 37, 43 and n, 49, 59, 99

"Do not disdaine, ô streight up raised pine . . .": 88

Dorus: 55, 56, 57, 58. *See also* Musidorus

"Dorus, tell me, where is thy wonted motion?": 52, 57, 58

double sestina: 12, 34, 44–45

"Doubt there hath bene . . ." (*A&S* 58): 93 n

"Doubt you to whom my Muse these notes intendeth?" (*A&S* 1st Song): 56, 73 n, 86

Drayton, Michael: 51

dream vision: 38. *See also* allegory

Du Bellay, Joachim: 13, 50, 51

Dyer, Edward: 13

Eglogs, Epytaphes, and Sonettes: 27 n

Elyot, Sir Thomas: 65, 66

energia: 69. *See also* rhetoric

epic: 48

Erasmus, Desiderius: 4–5, 65, 67, 72

espanados: 31, 33 n

epizeuxis: 33 n

euphuism: 18, 70, 72

"Faire eyes, sweet lips, deare heart . . ." (*A&S* 43): 85, 113

Symmetry and Sense

"Leave me ô love . . ." (CS): 105, 117–118

Leicester, Robert Dudley, Earl of: 9

"Let daintie wits crie on the Sisters nine . . ." (A&S 3): 69 n, 71, 112

Lever, Ralph: 65–66

"Like divers flowers . . .": 56, 88–89

"Like some weake Lords . . ." (A&S 29): 112

Lipsius, Justus: 5

"Locke up, faire liddes . . .": 87–88

logic: 5, 40–42, 43, 65 and n, 66, 75, 87–90, 94, 96, 97

"Lord, how do they encrease . . ." (Psalm III): 21

"Lord lett not mee a worm by thee be shent . . ." (Psalm VI): 22

love: in Ronsard and others, 51; in Renaissance poetry, 48–49, 69; in Sidney's work, 7, 52, 56, 61–62; in the Arcadia, 48, 55, 59–60; in Astrophel and Stella, 55, 70, 77, 78, 99–118. See also courtly love; Petrarchism; Plato; Platonism

"Love borne in Greece . . ." (A&S 8): 91, 112

"Love by sure proofe I may call thee unkind . . ." (A&S 65): 93 n

love melancholy: 60–62, 105 n, 116 n, 117

"Love's Progress": 37

"love which is imprinted in my soule . . ., The": 25–26

"Loving in truth, and faine in verse my love to show . . ." (A&S 1): 69 n, 79, 83–85, 93, 105 n, 112

merismus: 31

metaphor: 39, 45, 46, 68, 69

Metaphysical poets and poetry: 6, 67 n, 74, 88

meter: 22–23, 26–29, 43, 84

mimesis. See imitation

Montaigne, Michel de: 5, 68

Montemayor, Jorge de: 59

"Morpheus, the lively sonne of deadly sleepe . . ." (A&S 32): 112

"Muses, I oft invoked your holy ayde . . ." (A&S 55): 69 n

Musidorus: 52, 53, 55, 56, 57, 58, 62

"My God, my God, why hast thou me forsaken . . ." (Psalm XXII): 24

"My mouth doth water . . ." (A&S 37): 102

"My Muse may well grudge at my heav'nly joy . . ." (A&S 70): 85–86

"My muse what ail's this ardour . . .": 15 n

"My sheepe are thoughts . . .": 87

"My suite is just, just Lord . . ." (Psalm XVII): 21

"My true love hath my hart . . .": 35–36

"My words I know do well set forth my mind . . ." (A&S 44): 69 n, 113

"My words, in hope to blaze my steadfast minde . . .": 119 n

Nashe, Thomas: 101, 118–119

"neighbor mine not long ago there was . . ., A": 75

neoclassicism: 72

Nichomachean Ethics: 104–105

"No more, my deare . . ." (A&S 64): 93 n, 114

Nosce Teipsum: 75

"Not at the first sight . . ." (A&S 2): 83, 110

"Now that of absence the most irksome night . . ." (A&S 89): 11 and n

"Now was our heav'nly vaulte deprived of the light . . .": 38

"Nymph of the gard'n . . ." (A&S 82): 93 n

"O deare life, when shall it be . . ." (A&S 10th Song): 93, 95

"O eyes, which do the Spheares of beautie move . . ." (A&S 42): 42, 85, 89

"O Faire, ô sweete, when I do looke on thee . . ." (CS): 57

130

"O fate, ô fault, ô curse . . ." (*A&S* 93): 93 n, 95

"Of Imitation": 13 n, 65

Of the Knowledge which Maketh a Wise Man: 66

"Of this high grace with blisse conjoyn'd . . .": 60

"Oft with true sighes . . ." (*A&S* 61): 93 n, 115

"O Grammar rules . . ." (*A&S* 63): 93 n

"O happie Tems . . ." (*A&S* 103): 90–91

"O how the pleasant aires of true love be . . ." (*A&S* 78): 93 n

"O joy, too high for my low stile to show . . ." (*A&S* 69): 85–86

"O kisse, which doest those ruddie gemmes impart . . ." (*A&S* 81): 85–86

old *Arcadia:* 16, 119

"O Lord, my God, thou art my trustfull stay . . ." (Psalm VII): 21

"O Lord that rul'st our mortall lyne . . ." (Psalm VIII): 22, 23

"O my thoughtes, sweete foode my onely owner . . .": 15 n

"On *Cupids* bow how are my heartstrings bent . . ." (*A&S* 19): 79, 111, 112

"Onely Joy, now here you are . . ." (*A&S* 4th Song): 62, 86

Orator: 30, 68–69

oratory: 65–66, 67. *See also* poetry and oratory

"O sweet woods . . .": 15 n

"Out traytour absence . . ." (*A&S* 88): 116

"Over these brookes trusting to ease mine eyes . . .": 32–33

"O you that heare this voyce . . ." (*A&S* 6th Song): 73 n, 115

Pamela: 53

pastoral: 18, 19, 45, 46, 48, 55, 79, 82, 119

pathetic fallacy: 45, 87

Percy, William: 56 n

personification: 8, 25–26, 31, 40–43, 46; in *Arcadia* poems, 40, 90, App. C; in *Astrophel and Stella,* 73, 75, 90–96, 108; in *Certaine Sonets,* App. C

Petrarch, Francis: 49, 50, 51, 52, 54, 70, 73, 77, 91, 99, 109, 118

Petrarchism: 4, 6, 7, 42, 48–54, 56–57, 59, 61, 69, 70, 72, 73, 77, 79, 89, 91, 99, 100, 102, 103, 109, 117, 118. *See also* courtly love; love; anti-Petrarchism

"*Phaebus* farewell, a sweeter Saint I serve . . .": 41, 55

Phaedo: 105 n, 109 n

Phaedrus: 50–51, 52 n, 103, 108 n, 109

Philebus: 105 n

Philisides: 37

Philoclea: 59

"*Phoebus* was Judge betweene *Jove, Mars,* and *Love* . . ." (*A&S* 13): 91, 112

Plato: 50–51, 52, 103, 104, 105 n, 108 n. *See also* love; Petrarchism

Platonism: 7, 49, 50–53, 97, 107–110, 113. *See also* love; Petrarchism

Pléiade: 13, 51

ploce: 33 n, 81 n

poetry: ethical relevance of, 1; and music, 6, 13–15, 18, 27, 28; and oratory, 4, 12–13, 23, 28, 31, 34, 65, 68–69, 74–75, 81, 83, 87, 92, 94. *See also* meter; quantitative meter

"Ponder the wordes O Lord . . ." (Psalm V): 21, 22

premier livre des amores, Le: 56 n

prolepsis: 31

prosonomasia: 81 n

Psalms of David, The: 2, 7, 9, 10, 20–26, 44, 64, 73, 74, 77

Puttenham, George: 4, 12, 15 n, 18, 30–31

Pyrocles: 52, 58, 59, 62

quantitative meter: 13–19; Anacreontic, 15 n; Aristophanic, 15 n, 18–19; Asclepiadean, 15 n; elegiac distich, 15 n; hexameter, 14 n, 15–18; Phalacean hendecasyllable, 15 n; Sapphic, 15 and n, 16

"Queene *Vertues* court, which some call Stellas face . . ." (*A&S* 9): 80 n, 112

Raleigh, Sir Walter: 4
Ramus, Peter: 66–67
"Reason, in faith thou art well serv'd . . ." (*A&S* 10): 93 and n, 94, 106–107, 110
"Reason, tell me thy mind . . .": 15 n, 52
Republic: 105 n
rhetoric: 3–5, 7–8, 16, 17, 18, 20, 23, 28, 30, 32–36, 40, 43, 62, 63, 65 and n, 66, 67, 72, 74, 75, 80, 81, 82, 85, 86, 95, 96, 98. *See also* energia; style
rhetorical figures: 72, 74, 75, 78, 80. *See also* App. A; anadiplosis; anaphora; anthypophora; antithesis; asyndeton; blazon; climax; the collectour; epanados; epizeuxis; hirmus; merismus; ploce; prolepsis; prosonomasia; syllepsis; synathroesmus
rhythm: 3, 5, 11, 12, 15, 18–19, 23–29, 30, 33, 35–36, 43, 44–45, 48, 63, 67, 68, 70, 73, 74, 75, 78, 79, 80, 82, 84, 85, 86, 90, 96, 98. *See also* meter; quantitative meter; poetry, and music
Rich, Robert, 3rd Baron Rich: 112 n
"Ring out your belles . . ." (*CS*): 27–29, 62
Romantic poets: 72 n
Ronsard, Pierre de: 13, 50, 51, 56 n, 71 n, 118
Rule of Reason, The: 5 n

satire: 48
"Save me Lord, for why thou art . . ." (Psalm XVI): 21, 23
Scholasticism: 108–109 and n. *See also* Aquinas; Aristotle
Seneca: 68 n

sestina: 12, 41, 44–45
sestina, double: 12, 34, 44–45
Shakespeare: 43 and n, 77, 78, 98, 99, 103, 109 n, 116
"Shepheards tale no height of stile desires . . . , A": 79 n
"She comes, and streight therewith her shining twins do move . . ." (*A&S* 76): 78–79
Sidney, Sir Henry: 117 n
Sidney, Sir Philip: contemporary reputation of, 1; influence of, on other poets, 1, 6, 77, 119–120; on style, 1, 68–72, 82–83; modern criticism of, 2–3, 6, 13–14, 20–21, 44–45, 70, 73 and n, 74, 77, 78 n, 86, 91, 98, 99, 101–104, 109 n, 112 n, 117, 118; dating of poems of, 9 and n, 10; development of style of, 9–10, 119; experimental poems of, 9–19, 24, 28, 29, 36; use of song by, 24–28; interest of, in Ramism, 66–67; on translating Cicero, 66 n. *See also* titles of individual poems.
similitude: 69, 88
"Since natures workes be good . . ." (*CS*): 75, 105
"Since so mine eyes are subject to your sight . . .": 31
"Since that the stormy rage of passions darcke . . .": 11
"Since wayling is a bud of causefull sorowe . . .": 11
"Some Lovers speake when they their Muses entertaine . . ." (*A&S* 6): 69 n; 112
sonnet: 3, 48. *See also* Italian sonnet
Sonnets to the Faire Coelia: 56 n
"Soules joy, bend not those morning starres from me . . ." (*A&S* 48): 58, 85
Sowthern, John: 51
Spenser, Edmund: 4, 5, 13, 34, 48, 51, 73 and n, 98, 118; *Amoretti,* 51 n, 87 and n, 101
"Steele Glasse, The": 27 n
Stella: 56, 72, 91, 92, 94, 95, 101, 102, 103, 104, 107, 109, 110, 112–117
"*Stella* is sicke . . ." (*A&S* 101): 93 n

134